C000172405

KING OF THE 'CALI'

A Lifetime in Rock 'n' Roll

Russ Sainty

ONE OF BRITISH ROCK 'N' ROLL'S FOUNDING FATHERS

Book Castle
PUBLISHING

First published November 2008
by Book Castle Publishing
2a Sycamore Business Park
Copt Hewick
North Yorkshire HG4 5DF

The right of Russ Sainty to be identified as the author of this work has been asserted by him in accordance with the Copyright, Designs and Patents Act, 1988.

ISBN 978 1 903747 94 0

Designed and typeset by Caroline and Roger Hillier, The Old Chapel Graphic Design
www.theoldchapelivinghoe.com

Printed in Great Britain by CPI Antony Rowe, Chippenham, Wiltshire

CONTENTS

Eddy Green on stage at the California Ballroom, 1960s. *Photo courtesy of Cliff Hawkins*

THE 'CALI'
A PERSONAL INTRODUCTION

Not even Eddy Green – the owner, developer, proprietor and promoter of "THE CALIFORNIA POOL BALLROOM" – could have imagined the impact and the legacy that his project would have, when the doors to The Ballroom first opened on the evening of 12th March 1960. Thankfully, I was there on that opening night, booked by Mr Green himself as one of the acts to perform and "strut our stuff". Like Eddy, as I very soon affectionately called him, I too had no idea that following my first appearance I would be performing at the 'Cali' for a total of SIX memorable years! Now, nearly 50 years on, I'm about to tell you my memories of those wonderful "heady" days – to include how I first came to the area, how I got started as a Rock 'n' Roll singer, and indeed my Rock 'n' Roll journey after my six years performing at the 'Cali'. This is topped off by my celebrating 50 years in show business, and perhaps most memorably, on September 18th 2006, when I became officially recognised as a part of British Rock 'n' Roll history, named as one of British Rock's "Founding Fathers", no less! Yes, something I'm extremely proud of, and I will explain all later.

But for the moment, please join me at the beginning where everything started. I hope you will find my story interesting as you share many of the memories. Come on now, let's do it together!

Sincerely yours,
Russ Sainty

ACKNOWLEDGEMENTS

Through those heady, early Rock 'n' Roll years, starting late 1957 to 1965, I would like to acknowledge and thank the following people:

Firstly, my parents, who at all times gave me their full support to become a singer with a Rock 'n' Roll group, even though, in the beginning, they must have had their doubts, knowing I had just completed my apprenticeship in horticulture!

Mr Mason, my boss at the Leyton Borough Council Nurseries in Oliver Road, Leyton E10, for his true support, having lectured me for around five years and nurtured my horticulture career in order that I passed my RHS exams and became a propagator for the nursery!

Mr and Mrs Joseph, whose son Laurie Jay was The Nu-Notes' first drummer; they allowed us to rehearse upstairs in their small terraced house in Stamford Hill during 1959!

Paul Lincoln (owner) and Tom Littlewood (door manager) of the famous 2 i's Coffee Bar in London's Soho, for allowing me to sing in what was a hotbed of aspiring Rock 'n' Rollers!

Tony Sheridan, musician, singer, guitarist, who was kind enough to always be around to give me a great guitar backing whilst I was singing at the 2 i's during 1958/59.

Rhet Stoller's parents: Julian for his tireless efforts to drive us all, everywhere, during 1959 to 1961, and his mother Ann for her kindness to me, always asking me to stay for a meal. We were also lucky enough to rehearse in their house and do many of our demo recordings. By the way, the "Match of the Day" theme was also first recorded in the cellar of their house at 13, Glaserton Road, Stamford Hill.

Mr Bob Griffin, Mrs Griffin and daughter Joy, who were our greatest "groupies" and on many occasions provided us with a banquet from the boot of their car, as did another lovely couple, namely Harry and Nellie, who lived at Gravesend; oh, how they loved a party! Dave Taberer, a regular at the 'Cali', who became a big fan of Russ Sainty and The Nu-Notes. He soon became a very good friend, and with his knowledge of electrical equipment he became our man to fix each and every breakdown that occurred. Dave later married Joy Griffin, (groupie), and we are still good friends to this day. Rosemary Smith, a Cali regular, who would stand in front of the stage, watching every word I sang; she became an integral part of running my fan club.

Derek Jolly, who in 1957/8 was manager of The Buddy Munro Five, the skiffle come rock group, who allowed me to sing with them in my local pub, The Antelope, Church Road, Leyton, London. Derek later ran my office; we were the first Pop Group in the UK to be a Ltd. Company, R.M.B.LTD., "R uss- R oy- R het- M el and B ernie.

Mr Ron King and Alex the Barber, who booked us for all our early Gigs in 1959/60.

Mr and Mrs Eddy Green, creators of the phenomenon in pop music, known as THE CALIFORNIA BALLROOM, Dunstable, Bedfordshire, without whom this particular story would not be. My thanks to them for their faith in me for six long years, and never did we have a cross word.

Ann Graham, my girlfriend up to 1965, who gave me her total and dedicated support. Having married Ann on March 6th 1965, her support and dedication to further my show business career through the years, and to this very day, has been and still is total.

And finally, to the thousands of wonderful fans I had during those early days as a Rock 'n' Roll singer, and in many cases some of those fans have stayed the course to this day; however, I now call them friends.

Thanks to you all,
Russ Sainty

"The Cottage" A series of photographs taken in 2006, showing the actual cottage where I lived
and the surrounding area of Woughton on the Green, near Bletchley, Bucks., this being the
place of my evacuation during the early days of the Second World War, 1940/41.

Chapter One

BIRTH OF A ROCK 'N' ROLL STAR

The date is 13th April 1936, the place, 27, Simonds Road, Leyton, London, E10. Isabell Ellen and Alfred Richard Sainty become the proud parents of a beautiful, healthy, bouncing baby boy. Yes indeed, this was where and when it all began for me, Alfred Charles Sainty. Of course, you my reader will almost certainly know me as Russ Sainty, and rightly so, and I will of course explain to you a little later in my story just how I became Russ.

As you may well imagine, living in London's East End, I did experience the Second World War, which at first, being very young, I thought was fun. But it wasn't too long before I started to realise, through I guess seeing my parents in fear and panic during the heavy German bombing raids, that war was indeed no fun at all, and I too was very frightened just to hear that distinctive whistling sound as the bombs fell all around us.

However, towards the end of the year 1940, like thousands of other kids, I was evacuated to the country, but in my case I was lucky enough to go with both my Mum and Dad, as my dear father had failed his Army medical and was therefore not called up to serve in His Majesty's Services. We went to a wonderful part of Buckinghamshire, near Bletchley, a small village called Woughton on the Green. We lived in a small cottage owned by a Mr King, who himself lived next door, with his farm yard to the rear of both cottages. Oh boy, I remember this all so vividly; our cottage was very draughty, with no electricity, but it was magical, a real chocolate box cottage. I guess by now, as we go into the year 1941, I should be at infant school, but in truth I'm sure I learned more by just helping my parents to live day to day. After a short time, I remember my Dad starting a new job with the Post Office, driving a small red van, and I also remember Dad always talking about Fenny Stratford, Woburn Sands and Newport Pagnall. I guess these were places that he would go to each day? At weekends, I would go out with my parents; we would be wrapped up warm with wellington boots on our

A view from the canal back across the green, with the cottage nestled amongst the trees on the right.

feet, with my Dad carrying a large cross-cut saw. We would make our way across The Green, over the canal, into Coffee Hall Lane, and then deep into the woods, where we would collect fallen branches and cut them up for logs for our big open fire. This was an extra special place for me, because Mum always told me that Rupert Bear lived in these woods with the gypsies; oh, this was such a magical place where my imagination could run wild. I was crazy about Rupert Bear and would wait for our newspaper to be delivered every day in order that my Mum could read to me the next episode in Rupert's life. Another wonderful memory I have was to wait each day for our baker to deliver the bread; he would always give me a delicious Apple Turnover. Mmm! I can taste it now! The canal, just across The Green from our cottage, was a fascinating place for a young boy. I would walk along the bank and wait to see a barge come along and go under the bridge, though always a little frightened as I imagined the bargeman was a gypsy, and might catch me, taking me away on the barge. I now know this to be The Grand Union Canal, where beautiful small blue flowers along its banks known as forget me nots intrigued me; even at age five years old, I was captivated by nature itself. I recall begging my parents to let me have a small garden area, where I was able to grow a crop of peas, which I tended for weeks until they were ready for picking and eating. One of my most outstanding memories is playing "Blind Man's Buff" under the big oak tree situated at the end of our lane in the middle of a junction with the road to Bletchley. Can't imagine doing that today. I would play under the tree whilst my parents went into the nearby pub called Ye Olde Swan.

My reason for telling you about my evacuation back in 1940/41 is simply because I find it interesting, intriguing, ironic, to think that this cockney boy should turn up some 19 years later, singing Rock 'n' Roll at The California Pool Ballroom, Dunstable, which is, I guess, only around a dozen miles away from Woughton on The Green. Well, let me bring this matter right up to date, because I can tell you that during September 2006, having started my story about my Cali years and knowing that my evacuation was in the same area, it was important for me to go back and try to find the cottage that I had lived in some 65 years previously, and that's precisely what I did. With the knowledge that the area is now Milton Keynes, my feelings were that perhaps the old cottages had been knocked down for road building or other development, but after arriving in nearby Simpson I was directed by a local man to the

The Grand Union Canal situated across The Green from our cottage.

The old "Oak Tree" standing in the middle of a road junction leading from The Green to Simpson and Bletchley.

village of Woughton on The Green. Suddenly I saw an old oak tree in the middle of a small road junction and to my left was the pub, Ye Old Swan. My heart was leaping all over the place and I felt a bit tearful; "yes, yes, yes," I shouted to my wife Ann, "this is the place and it's just as I remember it." We then drove slowly down a small lane called The Green, and in front of me I could see the big area of green and in the distance the bridge over the canal. "But wait," I shouted, "that's the very cottage I'm looking for." I just stopped the car, and sat in complete wonder. There was silence in our car while I tried to compose myself; all my memories came flooding back, my Mum and Dad, my Gran, my playing with the lad next door, so many memories. We drove on over to the canal, but I was disappointed to find that

the very woods where we would cut up and collect fire wood, where Rupert Bear and the gypsies lived, had now been built on. Oh dear. I then drove back to our old cottage and knocked on the front door. A lady in possibly her late seventies answered, and I immediately told her who I was and why I had made my approach, after which she started to

The local church.

talk. She told me that after my family left the place in late 1941 the cottage was taken over by staff from Bletchley Park decoding unit, and following their departure she had lived there ever since. I asked her permission to take photos of the cottage, after which I left, feeling so happy that I had at last found the place which holds such wonderful memories for me, and in the knowledge that the cottage is in a conservation area, and well worth a visit by anyone – it's fabulous.

left
The local pub,
Ye Olde Swan,
Woughton on the
Green.

right
Myself standing at
the gate of number
6 The Green.

A view taken in 2008 of The Antelope, my local pub at the time, situated in Church Road, Leyton, London, E10. This being the place of my very first ever public performance in August 1957 singing with skiffle group, The Buddy Munroe Five.

Chapter Two

AND NOW FOR A LIFE-CHANGING EXPERIENCE

OK Let us get down to the nitty-gritty, namely Rock 'n' Roll. Please join me in one giant leap from the year 1941 to the year 1957, where on the one hand, as a cockney kid, through no fault of my own I was a victim of the Second World War, and some 16 years on, late July 1957 and still with a military theme, I'm just about to be de-mobbed from doing two years' national service with Her Majesty's Royal Signals Regiment, which just goes to show that none of us know what is round the next corner. Life is full of surprises and they are not all good ones. There is no doubt that during my army service, while based in Germany, Rock 'n' Roll

above July 1956, showing myself, centre front row, with room mates at Catterick Camp. Photo taken during basic training having been called up for my National Service when I joined the Royal Signals Regiment.

top Alfie at home on a 48-hour leave, following my first month's basic training.

started to come into my life. I would listen intently to the radio, evenings and weekends, excited by a new music from America called Rock 'n' Roll. Artistes such as Bill Hayley, Elvis Presley, Gene Vincent, Fats Domino, Frankie Lymon, The Platters, and Little Richard, just to name a few. The music was different, exciting, happy, controversial and definitely revolutionary; it was something for all young people to identify with, which seemed to go hand in hand with first the Milk Bars, and then the Coffee Bars; it was "cool" and "hip" to have a "frothy coffee" and play a Bill Hayley record on the Juke Box! I just had to be a part of this music, and by August 1957 found myself singing with a skiffle come Rock 'n' Roll group in my local pub; let me explain in more detail.

Having only been de-mobbed from the Army for a few weeks, I went to my local pub called The Antelope, where I was tipped off about a very good group appearing every weekend. As I walked into the bar, I was hit by this wonderful guitar strumming music, complete with a tea-chest bass, and a guy playing a washboard with thimbles on his fingers; it was fantastic! I had never before been close up to a live band of any kind, and I just stood listening and staring. Wow! The group was called The Buddy Monroe Five and completely out of the blue I went over to Buddy and asked if I could sing with the group. "Hold on, Alfie boy," a little voice in my head was saying, but to my surprise Buddy agreed that, if I learned a song, I could sing with the group the following weekend. The next morning I realised what I had done and felt a bit stupid since I had never even sung in the bath, let alone with a group in public. Well, the following weekend I turned up, having bought myself a new £30 guitar and learned half of a song called "A White Sports Coat", and true to his word Buddy announced me on the small stage in the corner of the bar. Dripping nervous sweat, I managed to get through the song and everyone applauded and yelled for more!

Blimey! This is just unbelievable, I was thinking, a fantastic feeling which confirmed to me that for sure I wanted to be a Rock 'n' Roll singer. Later that night, when the boys had finished their session, I sat down with them and their girlfriends, and ordered a round of drinks. We discussed my performance, and Buddy then said to me, "Alfie, if you learn a few more songs and get your guitar chords up to speed, would you like to join us, on a regular basis, as our guest singer?" "Yes, Yes, Yes," I shouted, "I really want to do it, and thanks for asking me." We then arranged some rehearsal dates with their friend/manager, a Leyton lad called Derek Jolly, at which point one of the girlfriends said to me, "Alfie, have you ever thought about changing your name, because we all think that Alfie is not really a Rock 'n' Roll singer's name?" I said, "Well no, no, I haven't, things are all happening so fast, but I would be quite happy to do so." After about ten minutes, and going through dozens of names, the four girlfriends shouted, "RUSS, that's the one, you look like a Russ, what do you think of it, Alfie?" I said, "Yeh, sounds good to me, ok then, I'm now RUSS SAINTY. Ha Ha, I'd better go over and tell my parents and sister Brenda." With that we all said our good-nights, and I walked home with my family – with Russ as the topic of conversation, my Mum saying how hard it might be for her to get used to it, but she did like the name.

The next morning, I had to be up early for work. I was starting back at my old job, working

Derek Jolly, stage name Derek Day, manager of The Buddy Munroe Five 1957/8. In 1962 Derek also ran the small office in my house.

as a propagator in our local borough council's nursery. Yes, I was very apprehensive, as this would be my first day back after doing two years' National Service! But more worrying was the fact that I was now completely hooked by this new phenomenon in music called Rock 'n' Roll! However, I had no need to worry. My boss, my foreman and all the staff gave me a warm welcome, but I had to tell them straightaway that my name was now Russ and no longer Alfie. Everyone laughed and asked me what was going on, and why the change? Well, I decided to tell them the complete story, and strangely enough even my boss, Mr Mason, was interested and wished me well, together with everyone else. OK. It was a talking point for a day, but after that things settled down, and I was happy that I had got it off my chest and told them all, right from the start, so now let's get on with the job!

Russ practicing guitar chords whilst on holiday in Weymouth, summer 1958.

Chapter Three

IT'S NOW THE YEAR 1958

start this year off doing a few small shows with The Buddy Monroe Five, and by now I've learned a few more songs and a few more chords on the guitar. I'm not a proper member of the group, but they put me on as a sort of guest singer, which is fine by me. I decided to try and get a few bookings on my own and approached the manager of the Rialto Cinema in Leytonstone High Road, asking him if I could sing a few songs in between the films. Now this was unheard of at the time, but as luck would have it the manager agreed. I tried desperately to get a nice coloured shirt and some show biz type shoes, but to be honest it was a real struggle. Men's clothes in 1958 were still pretty drab, and the best I could get was a maroon and black check shirt; as for the shoes, that was a non-starter. I had asked our maintenance lads at work to make me an amplifier, in order that I could use the electric guitar, and the boys came up with the goods, a 30 watts amp. Wow! Laughable today, but at the time this was just perfect. It's Saturday night, and with my cousin Robert we make our way to the rear door of the cinema and meet up with the manager, who directs me to a power point for my amplifier, which unfortunately was a bit too far away, and I didn't have any kind of extension lead. Oh well, not to worry. I get changed and await my turn to go on a proper big stage for the first time in my life, and ALONE! I hear an announcement about a nice surprise for you all, and it ended with the words "please welcome Russ Sainty". I run on to the centre of the stage and, as I do so, I feel the connecting wire from the guitar to the amplifier snap! Oh No! Oh No!, then I do the worst thing possible and start apologizing, but have no option other than to try and carry on, with just an acoustic guitar which could hardly be heard. I do my five songs and get a sympathetic round of applause. I walk off stage, very upset, as it was like singing Rock 'n' Roll without any backing music. However, the manager was happy and offered me another spot, and this time I would get a £10 fee, yippee!

But before this, I'm going on a two-week holiday to Weymouth, where Mum and Dad have booked a caravan, and there is enough room for Robert my cousin to come. We have a smashing holiday, and Robert and I meet up with a couple of girls, and we exchange addresses, like you do! (remember, it's 1958). On my return back home, I contact Buddy Monroe and ask him, would he give me some group accompaniment for my next show and he was delighted to have the opportunity and said, "Russ, let's do some Rockin'." I would have two electric guitars and tea chest bass, didn't have any drums, only a skiffle wash board, which I decided against. To think that it's only a matter of months since I was asking Buddy if I could sing with him, and here we are, with him giving me a backing on a real stage. The night came for us to do the show and I have to say, it was fantastic, I felt like I had made it, the audience gave us tremendous applause, and I got paid a tenner!

My pride and joy, that little Ford Thames Van I bought during 1958.

It's now around early August, and I go with my Dad to a garage in Croydon, where I'm about to pick up my new purchase; it's a lovely little Ford Thames van, just a year old, and has been re-sprayed. It's an ex Singer sewing machine van. They used to sell them off cheap, after one year, as they had to buy a fleet of new ones. It only cost £300, and to this day it's one of the best vehicles that I've ever had, and it never ever let me down. At last I was able to get around, and one of my first trips was to Tadworth, near Epsom in Surrey. I had gone looking for the girl that I met on holiday in Weymouth, and yes, I found the house, knocked on the door and who should answer it but Valerie, who was in total shock that I had gone to see her!

This was to be the start of a relationship that lasted about eight months, a first for both of us, and we had a lot of fun together, but things were about to change. I saw an advertisement for singers and acts to audition for the famous Carol Levis Discovery Show, and I decided to make enquiries. I'm told to go to a theatre in Hammersmith, where I would have to audition, and, playing guitar, I sang the Everly Brothers' hit "All I Have to do is Dream". The audition went really well, and I was later informed that I had passed and would be appearing at the Finsbury Park Empire. This was fantastic news, just to think that I will be performing on a stage that over the years will have seen all the top performers of the day; this for me would be something very special, and I was so looking forward to doing it. The big night came, and I had the support of all my family, aunts and uncles included, and believe me I needed them. For the first time I was quite nervous, and I remember my Mum saying "get yourself a brandy to settle your nerves." There were about fifteen acts, all doing about three minutes on stage. The atmosphere was wonderful, and I felt like I was really in show business! It was now my turn to go on and do my number. Mr Levis gave me a big introduction, and I walked on to the centre of the stage to a stand microphone and sang my heart out. Mr Levis walked on and asked the audience for their applause as I walked off stage. Oh what a thrill that was. I was so happy that I had done a good performance. Later, when all the acts had been on, we were all brought back on stage, and Carol Levis asked the audience for applause for each act, and the noise would be recorded on what was called the Clapometer. No, I'm not joking, that's how it was judged. No, I didn't win, but that didn't bother me at all. I was more than happy just to have been on the show, a great experience, I have to say!

It's now end of August/September time 1958, and I hear about how Tommy Steele had started his career in a small coffee bar in Soho's Old Compton Street, London. It was called the 2 i's Coffee Bar and owned by a wrestler called Paul Lincoln. I had a chat with my parents and asked them what they thought about me going to find the place, and perhaps try my luck in London's West End. Now, you have to realise that I was an East End boy, and, though only about eight miles away, the West End of London was worlds apart. It might as well have been a thousand miles away, and at the age of twenty two I had only ever been to Selfridges, in Oxford Street, to see Father Christmas, as a young boy. Well, it was decided that I go and look for this small coffee bar, and my Dad would come with me. Which is what we did. Having found the place, we parked outside, (no yellow lines or parking meters then), and I walked in with my guitar and asked for the person in charge. As I stood waiting, I looked at all the photos on the back wall, Tommy Steele, The Vipers Skiffle Group, Terry Dean, Lonnie Donegan, and quite a few others. The place was small, but full of young people sitting on stools at quite a high counter. There was a fantastic smell of coffee and a gushing sound from the machines behind the counter. The place was buzzing with a very up-beat feel. I had never experienced this before and I was quite overwhelmed by it all. Suddenly, a well-built man came up to me and said, "Hello, who are you?" I said, "I'm Russ Sainty, I'm a Rock 'n' Roll singer, and play guitar." He said, "OK, let's see what you can do," and took me down a very small staircase to a basement, which at one end had a small stage and at the other end, high up in the corner, was a metal grill. I was able to see people's feet walking past on the pavement outside. He switched on the sound system and said to me, "I'm Tom Littlewood, the manager here, and if I like what you do, I'll give you a spot down here. OK, let's hear you then." I sang a couple of songs and he stopped me and said "Yeh, Yeh, Yeh, OK, your singing is alright, but I think you would be better without that guitar, hang on a minute." He then called a young fellow down from up in the Coffee Bar and told him to give me a decent guitar backing. The young fellow turned out to be Tony Sheridan. We chose a song and away we went. It was fantastic. His guitar work behind me was inspirational, I will never forget it! Tom Littlewood then stopped us and said,"OK, OK, yeh, that's good, very good, you can come down here and sing whenever you want, and Tony will give you a backing." I thank Tom and Tony, make my way up the stairs and rush out to find Dad waiting in my van. Dad said to me, "How'd you get on mate?" I said, "Dad, it was just magic, and Tom said that I can sing down there whenever I want, and I've got a great guitarist to back me, called Tony Sheridan." Dad said, "Is he going to pay you?" I said, "No, Dad, but I'm not bothered about that. I just want to be seen and discovered." We drove home and told my Mum and sister Brenda, who were both very excited at me singing in the West End. However, I suddenly thought about the next morning. I would be back at work and I was concerned that, with such a responsible job, would I now be able to mix the two things, Rock 'n' Roll and horticulture, a bit like oil and water!

It wasn't too long before my boss, Mr Mason, got to know about my exploits at the 2 i's Coffee Bar and asked to see me. He was really nice about it, to my surprise, and wanted to know all about how I was getting on, and wished me luck. He then said to me, "Sainty, how would you like to sing in The Coronation Gardens Concert Hall, Leyton? And better still, I will authorise all the nursery staff to come down and see you perform." Bloody hell, I was completely flabbergasted, what a wonderful thing for him to do for me; but then that's the sort of man he was, what a boss, he was top man in every respect. Well, we arranged an afternoon for this to take place, and true to his word he arranged for all the staff to take their seats and watch me do about half a dozen songs. It was really embarrassing, and I felt more nervous than ever before, but all the staff loved what I did, and I was thrilled that at least now everyone knew what I was up to, and that the cat was truly out of the bag!

I now find myself going up to the 2 i's almost every night, and sometimes at weekends. It was like a drug to me. I was completely hooked on the magic and excitement of it all, and every night was different. My cousin Robert was still living with me, and most nights he would come with me; we were very very close. Most nights I would not get home until about midnight, and having to be up for work at 7am was getting to me. I was by now feeling the pressure of keeping all these balls in the air at the same time. Some mornings, I would be so tired that I would climb underneath the staging of my greenhouse, onto the hot pipes that heated the place, and drop off to sleep. On occasions, my foreman would come looking for me, walking past me as I lay sleeping on the hot pipes. Now this was not like me at all. I loved my job and was always completely committed and conscientious, and was feeling quite guilty at my behaviour. Something has gotta give sooner or later, I was thinking.

The 2 i's was small, hot and steamy, even though it was now winter time. The only fresh air to get in came through a small opening, high up in the right hand corner. However, the atmosphere was incredible. Playing on the tiny stage, for myself and a few others, would be a combination of the following: on drums, Tony Meehan, Brian Bennett or Red Rees, on bass was always Brian (Liquorice) Locking, on guitars, Tony Sheridan or Big Jim Sullivan, what a wonderful choice! Other regulars I would see most nights, who became good friends, were: Ian Samwell, (wrote "Move It"), Wee Willy Harris, Vince Taylor, The Most Brothers, (Micky Most), Terry Dean, Hank Marvin, Bruce Welch, Jet Harris, (The Drifters), Freddy Lloyd, (Vipers Skiffle Group), Larry Page and many more would visit, like Cliff Richard and Adam Faith, Vince Eager etc., etc. You may well wonder why there are no girls on the list above? Well, that's the way it was. I can't think of any English, female Rock 'n' Roll singers at this time.

I also met another very well know person, one cold wet December night, just before Christmas. His name was Lionel Bart, no less! I had just finished doing a twenty-minute spot with Tony Sheridan, Tony Meehan and Brian Locking backing me, and Lionel Bart, who was in the audience, called me over and said," Russ, let's get out of here, I want to speak to you." We pushed our way through the crowded cellar and up that tiny staircase, then out into the fresh air. Wow! Lionel suggested we go across the road to another quiet coffee bar called Act One Scene One, or a name very similar. With my

Russ with cousin Robert, both dressed to kill and on their way to a local gig, 1958.

cousin Robert, we sat down with Mr Bart and he ordered three coffees, and then said to me, "Russ, I think you're very good, and I believe I've got a song that would be just perfect for you to record?" I said, "Yeh, Yeh, that's what I want, yes I desperately want to make a record!" He then said, "Listen, why don't you both come back to my place tonight and we can run it through." Blimey, what an offer, I'm thinking, and then suddenly I went all protective and started to remember what my uncle Alf had told me. "Watch out for them

queers and poofs in the West End." So I naively and stupidly said to Lionel, "Ah, Ah, well, I'd like to, but I've got to be up early for work in the morning," and nervously stood up and said, "We had better go now, but thanks for coffee." How pathetic was that, I ask you? And I was 22 years old. I know this must be hard to believe, but it's absolutely true. Question is, did I blow that one chance I was looking and hoping for? Only time will tell!

Chapter Four

MEET RUSS SAINTY AND THE NU-NOTES

It's January, and things are going well for me. I'm still at the 2 i's and Tom Littlewood is now sending me out on small gigs with Tony Sheridan, Brian Locking and Tony Meehan. Two of these gigs stand out in my mind, and for completely different reasons. The first one being a booking at Trowbridge in Wiltshire. We all pile into my little Ford Thames van, with Brian's double bass tied on top, and off we go. I guess it was about a hundred miles from London, but we were there in good time. The gig was either at the Town Hall or The Corn Exchange. We kicked off with Tony doing about 45 minutes, and then I did about half an hour. The kids went wild. It was complete chaos, believe me. You have to remember, this was the first time ever for these kids to see someone singing LIVE ROCK 'N' ROLL, and there was hysteria all round us. Following the show, we all piled back into my van and set off for London. It was a freezing cold night, and my van, like most others in those days, did NOT have any form of heater! Well, after only a few miles, our breath was freezing up on the windscreen and my fingers on the steering wheel went numb. Tony was huddled up in the front passenger seat, and poor Brian Locking was curled up in a ball, lying in the back. Meanwhile I was trying desperately to rub a hole in the ice to enable me to see where I was going. The journey was a nightmare, but we finally made it to London about 7am when I dropped the boys off. Oh, what a trip!

A week or so later, we were doing a similar gig in a London club, and having just finished my spot with the Conway Twitty hit song "It's Only Make Believe", as I walk off stage two young guys stop me in my tracks, telling me how good they thought I was, and introduce themselves as Laurie Jay

Winter 1958, a rare photo of Tony Sheridan, the occasion being a gig at Trowbridge Town Hall that Tom Littlewood, manager of the 2 i's Coffee Bar, had booked for Tony, myself and Brian (Liquorice) Locking. The show was great but our trip home was not so good, we almost froze to death!

(Joseph) and Barry Stoller. They said I would be perfect for their group called The 4 Teens, who desperately needed a singer, and would I be interested in joining them? I said, "Let's swap phone numbers, and I'll think about it." To be honest, I didn't think much more about it, but the next evening Laurie phoned me up and talked me into going over to see the boys playing. It was only at Stamford Hill, about 20 minutes drive from Leyton. I found Laurie's house, and he welcomed me in, introducing me to his Mum and Dad first, and then taking me upstairs, where I was introduced to the other members of The 4 Teens. The full line-up was Laurie Jay (Drums), Barry Stoller (Lead Guitar), Mel Miller (Double Bass) and Stanley Jellan (Rhythm Guitar and Singer). "Do you want to hear us, Russ?" Laurie shouted to me. "Yes mate, go for it," and they went into a good up-tempo rock number called "Twenty Flight Rock", and they sounded really good. I was impressed immediately. We then decided that I should try a few songs with them, the very first being "It's Only Make Believe". As we finished the number, we all looked at each other for a reaction and smiled. A few seconds passed and I said, "Boys, that was great!" We then go straight into a song, and now it's getting very loud. Laurie was so heavy on the drums, and Barry had turned up his lead guitar. We were really rockin', and all this in small terraced house. With that, Laurie's Mum brought up some tea and sandwiches, so we stopped for some nosh and a chat. The question put to me was, would I join them? I said, "Fellows, I'd love to be a part of the group, but only on condition that I retain my full name, Russ Sainty." Now these boys were all Jewish and by nature would not want to give too much away, and would do their utmost to get the best deal possible, which was OK by me, but I too was not about to give way when it came to my name. Their concern was that, should I be a success, I may well walk away from the group at some stage, so we decided to give it some breathing space before any firm decisions were made, because deep down I knew that they needed me more than I needed them, but I also knew that if I made the commitment to join them, I would not simply walk away.

I continue to go to the 2 i's for a week or so, and recall one particular evening when myself and Wee Willy Harris decided to get a taxi and go to see Cliff Richard and The Drifters performing at the Hammersmith Gaumont. Remember, by this time Cliff had already had a big hit with his first record, "Move It", composed by one time member of The Drifters, Ian Samwell. The show was great, Cliff performing in a pink jacket. I'll never forget that, nor will I forget the reaction of all the girls in the audience. They were going wild and screaming the place down. It was fabulous. This is what it's all about, I was thinking. After the show, Wee Willy and myself didn't have enough dosh for a cab, so decided to walk all the way back to Soho, where for some reason I had left my van, parked outside the 2 i's. Can you imagine, walking through London with a little short man with bright red hair. That was Willy, and in those days this was quite outrageous! We finally made it back, but it was a bloody long walk.

Work for me at the nursery was still going along fine, and I still loved my job, even though I was very tired some mornings after a late night/early morning gig. I should also mention that I was no longer seeing my girlfriend Valerie. It was all getting too much for me, and I was not ready for a serious relationship. She and her family were very nice people, and I hope that life has been, and still is, kind to them. The last I heard was that Valerie had married a cockney guy and they had a little boy, but that was a long long time ago, how time flies.

Through the grapevine, I heard about a group playing at a pub called The Lion and Key, just up the road from our house in Leyton High Road. I decided to have a night off and went to see what they were like; as it happens, they were very good. It turned out to be Joe Brown and the Bruvvers, and over the next few months I got to know the boys very well. Joe worked on the railways, and very often would turn up for the gig straight from work on his motor bike, still dressed in his leathers! The Bruvvers lived in Frances Road Leyton, where their parents had a small corner shop, which I think was a newsagent's. Strangely enough, I've not met up with Joe since those days at the pub in 1959. Yes, our paths have crossed over the years, but somehow we always seem to miss each other on the road!

By now, I've met up with The 4 Teens a few times for rehearsals, and a group name has been decided by the boys. They want to be known as The Nu-Notes, and I will keep my own name, so from now on, we will be known as Russ Sainty and The Nu-Notes. I decide to stop going to the 2 i's Coffee Bar, and start serious rehearsal with the boys. Mr Joseph and Mr Stoller between them will act as our manager and also provide us with transport, my little van being far too small, of course. After about three weeks, we had enough material to do about 40 minutes. Thankfully, Mr Joseph knew a hairdresser in Tottenham, who, together with another guy called Ron King, was putting on dance gigs in all the small halls for miles around, and having done one booking for them, we then did every hall that they promoted – to name a few, Hendon, High Barnet, Romford, Bletchley and many more. Apart from these dance gigs, there were really only the package tours, so these were our audience, unlike the massive concerts of today. Some of our supporting groups were The Dave Clark Five, Chris Farlowe, Rory Storm and many more. I recall

1959, Russ in full flow, rock on!

that Chris Farlowe always looked poorly, very pale, and sounded like he had a bad cold. I also remember that his drummer was terrific; sorry, can't recall his name.

As the weeks go by, we are getting a very good reputation, and had regular bookings every week, things were going great! Then, at a rehearsal upstairs in Laurie Jay's house, Stan Jellan, rhythm guitarist and backing vocals, made the decision that he no longer wanted to continue as a member of The Nu-Notes and would leave after the weekend. What do we do now, having got bookings for two months ahead? I think his nose was put out when I took over as lead singer; oh well, that's life, it's his loss, as I'm sure we can get someone to take his place. Mel said he knew a young lad who had just started playing guitar and lived opposite him. "I'll try to make contact with him," Mel said. Well, a day or two later Mel brings a young lad along to Laurie's house for a rehearsal; his name Roy Toft. He only had a tiny amplifier and, having run through a few songs, it was pretty obvious he was not very good. Even I could play more chords than him, and I was pretty poor, oh dear what now? Well, we told Roy to do a lot of practice and we would try again, and to his credit a week later he had improved by a mile and the boys took him on as a member of The Nu-Notes! As I was to learn over the years, Roy was a great tryer, very determined, and always delivered. He was also able to sing, which was another good point. We do a few gigs with Roy, and the group are back, rockin' better than ever and by now we can do at least one hour of good material.

Here comes another bombshell! Laurie Jay makes his announcement. He has decided to leave The Nu-Notes! What the hell's going on with you lot? I was thinking, but it wasn't too long before I could see the problems. Laurie's Dad wanted his son to be a star and Barry's Dad wanted his son to be a star.

And we had weeks of arguments between the two fathers! Had they forgotten about me fronting the group? The arguments continue, and now Mel Miller's Dad gets involved, but most of this is going on behind my back. However, it now seems that much of this bad feeling is not only about each Dad wanting their son to be The Star. They were also concerned at me perhaps becoming a star. All this back stabbing and arguing was becoming too much for me, and I told the boys that if things didn't change for the better, I would consider leaving the group.

Things are all upside down for a week or so, until Barry phones to tell me that he has made contact with a young Jewish boy, who lives at Neasden, N.W. London, just off the North Circular Road; his name Bernie Martin. Rehearsals were arranged, and Bernie turned up with a drum kit that came

A rare 1959 photo of myself and the Boys showing our first drummer, second from left, Laurie Jay.

straight out of the ark. Bloody hell, I thought to myself, this is all a bit different to what I had been used to at the 2 i's, with Red Rees, Tony Meehan, Brian Bennett and the likes! However, Bernie was very good, and would probably sound much better on a decent drum kit. OK, let's go over The Nu-Notes' new line-up; it's now Barry Stoller, (lead guitar), Mel Miller, (bass), Roy Toft, (rhythm guitar), Bernie Martin, (drums). And of course, I'm fronting the group. Now, I have to tell you that at this time my mother had been admitted to a hospital in Brentwood, Essex, and was found to have TB (tuberculosis), and was very ill. It was decided that she was not well enough to have a lung removed, so would spend at least six months in hospital, being prepared until it was considered that she was well enough to have what was a big operation. During this time, with my Dad and sister Brenda, we kept the house going and drove to Brentwood most evenings when possible. This was indeed a tough time for us all, and it was during this time, which all in all lasted almost a year, that Mrs Ann Stoller was so kind to me! Whenever I arrived at 13, Glaserton Road, Stamford Hill, Barry's home, for rehearsals, she would always sit me down to have dinner with the family, and I have to say she was a good cook, and I had some smashing, memorable, Jewish dishes which I shall never forget. If you're looking down on us, Ann, I thank you so much for your kindness!

With a few good rehearsals under our belts, we go to the famous Max Rivers rehearsal rooms near Leicester Square, and audition for ex-band leader and booking agent, Mr Lou Preager, who considered us just perfect for doing cabaret at the American military bases situated in the South of England – to name a few, Mildenhall, Alconbury, Lakenheath etc. These gigs were a fantastic experience for us all, just imagine it! We were thrown in with all types of real show biz acts, and here we are, a mere Rock 'n' Roll pop group, with very little experience, topping the bill in these cabaret shows, week after week, and the yanks loved us!

We find ourselves busy all through the summer and into autumn, and it's only thanks to Mr Julian Stoller, Barry's Dad, that we were able to get about. Mr Stoller was a wholesaler for kippers, yes, the ones you eat! Almost every week, myself and the boys would make a chain from the van to Barry's front garden and unload boxes of kippers, then load the van with our equipment. Yes, it did smell a bit fishy at times, but Mr Stoller was a real gem, and would take us all over the place for gigs and auditions. The worst thing was, on our return home from a show, it might be say 3am, we would unload all our gear, then have to make a human chain as before to load all those smelly boxes of kippers back into the van; oh, the glamour of show biz.

NEWLY-FORMED BRITISH BAND FOR U.S. OFFICERS' CLUB IN TURKEY

NU-NOTES IMPRESS AMERICANS

FOR THE FIRST TIME EVER, a British band has been booked to play in Turkey.

And, what is even more unique, the band is not a name one; in fact, it is comparatively new, has had less than six months' professional experience.

But it now has a golden opportunity to make the Big Time.

For it is being boosted by two American military personnel, Sergeants Casker and Holmes, secretary and president of the Board of Governors N.C.O., respectively, of the Toppers Officers' Club in Ismia.

Sgts. Casker and Holmes heard the outfit during one of its engagements at an American camp in this country, immediately contacted the personal manager of the band, Bob Ashton, and in a short while a deal was made, contracts signed and all arrangement made for the band to leave for a guaranteed 90 days engagement in Turkey. . .

Name of the band is the NU-NOTES; it is a 5-piece, is made up as follows: MEL MILLER, of Stamford Hill, London, N., aged 19 (bass); BARRY STOLLER, 18, of Stamford Hill (guitar); RUSS SAINTY, the leader, 21, of Leytonstone, London, S., vocalist; ROY TOFT, 18, of Stamford Hill (rhythm guitar) and BERNARD MARTIN, 17, of Neasden, N.W. (drums).

They leave for Turkey early in January.

The Nu-Notes made their TV debut on the "Focus on Youth" programme, followed it with a week's variety at the Met., Edgware Road, then went on to play one-night engagements at the Pigalle, Cafe-de-Paris and other well-known restaurants.

Sgt. Casker evidently believes they have a lot of talent. "In fact," he told R. & S.M., "I was so impressed with their style, personality and musicianship that automatically I knew they'd be a cinch for our officers' club in Turkey".

Sgt. Holmes said: "I agree with my colleague. And, by the way, if this British band goes over well with the members of our club in Turkey, we shall be seeking out similar outfits and be interested also in booking package shows."

July 1959

Opening night at The 59 Club, Hackney East London, showing Russ with some happy fans and Father Oates looking on. In the background are my cousin Robert and two of my best army mates, Ted and Barney Winkley.

It's autumn, and I'm contacted by a Father Oates from Hackney, a couple of miles down the road from my home in Leyton. It seems that he had heard of us and tracked me down. He wanted us to do a gig at his new club for teenagers, at a big church hall called Eton Mission, Hackney Wick, East London. I will never forget that first night we played at Eton Mission. Mr Stoller had driven us to Hackney, where we met Father Oates in the court yard, and he then said to us, "Hello boys, welcome to Eton Mission, you will be playing upstairs in the big hall, and by the way the club is called The 59 Club." Well, by about 7.30pm the place was heaving with young and very excited teenagers. We played our first session and brought the house down! The kids went mad at every hip movement I made. Back stage was my cousin Robert and two of my best army mates, Barney and Ted Winkley, who lived at The Elephant and Castle. During our break, dozens of young girls forced their way back stage, where I was mobbed by them. It was a wonderful time, and to be honest I really felt like a Rock 'n' Roll star. Well, like all good things the evening came to an end, but Father Oates was so happy, and booked us for many more dates, including the official opening of the club in a few weeks' time!

Now it was around this time that a certain Malcolm Rose, from Ilford in Essex, came onto the scene as our manager, and he promised all sorts of things including getting us on TV! And true to his word, within a couple of weeks he had arranged for us to do our first television show for the BBC. It was live and was broadcast from the Beeb's Wembley studio. I can't recall the name of the programme, but I can recall that we were rubbish. Being completely inexperienced, having never done any TV, I listened intently to the floor manager, who instructed me to start singing when I saw the red light on the camera. Meanwhile, the Nu-Notes had already started playing, with me still standing like a fool, waiting for this bloody red light! Well, as you can imagine when it did finally come on and I did finally start singing, the Nu-Notes were well into the song, hence, they were in one part of the song

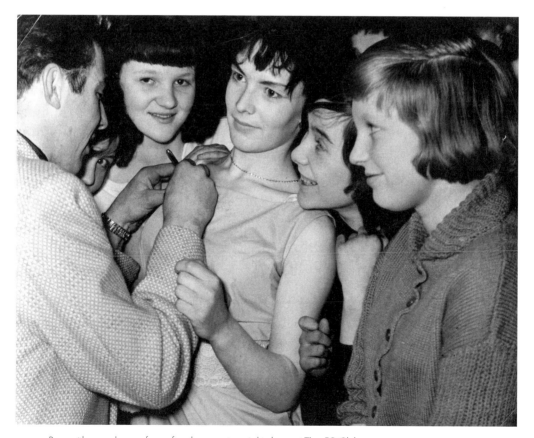

Russ with more happy fans after the opening night show at The 59 Club.

and I was in another! Oh dear, live TV. However, somehow we did all finish together. The song by the way was called "Teenager in Love", a hit for Marty Wilde and my best show biz buddy to this day, Craig Douglas.

Now, on the subject of television, the show "Six Five Special", which started in the year 1957, had now for a couple of years been the most exciting thing for young people on The Box. I can see the likes of Pete Murray, Josephine Douglas and Don Lang in my mind's eye to this day. However, next year, 1958, producer Jack Goode brought to our front rooms the fabulous show called "Oh Boy". This was transmitted at about 6pm every Saturday night live! I would think that almost everyone with a television set switched on to this show, which was so exciting even the adults were now beginning to enjoy Rock 'n' Roll. The big band was led by Harry Robinson and called Lord Rockingham's XI, with such musicians of the day as Rocking Rex Morris (tenor sax), Eric Ford (lead guitar), Cherry Wainer (keyboards and resident vocal), and dance groups such as The Dallas Boys and the glamorous, leggy Vernon Girls. These, together with the fantastic big band sound, would accompany such acts as Cliff Richard and The Drifters (Shadows), Marty Wilde, Dickie Pride, Tommy Edwards, Joe Brown, Neville Price and the Cutters, Little Tony, Michael Cox, Cuddly Dudley and Gene Vincent etc. Things on the telly are moving fast, because this year, 1959, will see the birth of another Rock 'n' Roll show called "Boy Meets Girl", an up-beat, fast, exciting show which was to be the making of Marty Wilde, and "Drumbeat" was a show that made such acts as Adam Faith and Vince Eager.

There is no doubt that 1959, though disruptive with group personnel, was a big year for us as Russ Sainty and The Nu-Notes. We were by now a known and respected group, and just needed a little push from someone to become a household name. However, though we were busy, it was because of the input of myself and Mr Stoller, not from any efforts by our manager Malcolm Rose, so we decided to sack him and carry on doing things ourselves for the time being.

It was now becoming extremely hard for me personally. Remember, I still had a very responsible job, producing thousands of plants for both Leyton and Leytonstone Borough Councils. I also had my mother in hospital, and she had now had a massive operation to take away her infected lung, and our visits to her hospital in Brentwood were at least 20 miles away. I was also doing private garden and tree work with my foreman, Jackie Boyd, my dad and my cousin Robert, so it was a very busy time, but let me stress, apart from my poor mum being very ill, everything else was just fine, and it was a very exciting time. I loved the buzz of it all.

Earlier in the year, we did an audition for Jack Goode's "Oh Boy" show, and though he liked us, we never did get onto the show; this was a great disappointment, I have to say. But I did get a call from Father Oates of Hackney's 59 Club, at Eton Mission, who confirmed a date for the official opening of the club, (sorry can't recall the date); he also told me that the club would be opened by none other than Princess Margaret and Cliff Richard, and that we would be the supporting group. Well, I have to tell you, this official opening night was just fantastic. No, I didn't get to meet any royalty, but following Cliff on stage, who by the way only did a couple of songs, Russ Sainty and The Nu-Notes completed the evening, and we had a ball, the young girls just screaming for most of our set; this was indeed Rock 'n' Roll! Following this successful evening and the fan worship we had built up, Father Oates and Father Bill Shergold commissioned us to make a private 45 record single, especially for all club members to purchase. A date was fixed, and off

Photo showing the private single we recorded for The 59 Club, year 1959, hence the club name.

we went with Father Oates to HMV Studios, above a shop in Oxford Street, London, and we recorded two numbers, namely "Too Much", an Elvis Presley hit, and "One of These Mornings", a hit song for Ricky Nelson. The recording completed and the vinyls pressed, we then attended a launching of the single down at the club, with the record being blasted out over the sound system, and us just sitting selling records and signing autographs. It was a great evening for everyone, and guess what; I've still got a copy of the record. Father Oates was full of good ideas, and next he was to organise a train trip to Clacton on Sea, all club members and parents being invited for this day trip to the seaside. And guess what, he booked Russ Sainty and The Nu-Notes to play Rock 'n' Roll on both the outward and return journeys. We set up in a massive, specially prepared empty carriage, electricity was provided for our equipment, and we rocked all the way to Clacton, with the kids jiving and having great fun. Oh, what a day it turned out to be. We even made the daily newspapers, which was a first, and I personally was thrilled to be a part of it!

1959, my first studio photo, a definite improvement on the other one. (1960s)

As the 1950s come to an end, there is a young people's mini revolution erupting and about to burst out onto the scene. Let me sum up my '50s of hope, opportunity and optimism, following those dark days of war. I have embraced hope, taken opportunities and I'm very optimistic. I have tried to become a jockey, I've served an apprenticeship in horticulture, I've been a soldier, and I'm a Rock 'n' Roll singer, and part of the new young people's music revolution, so for me the fabulous fifties have been a wonderful time. LET'S KEEP ROCKIN'!!

My first give away post card photo; note my autograph, it did improve, honest!

Chapter Five

OPENING NIGHT
AT THE 'CALI'

The '60s for most people will be remembered for many reasons, and I will list just some of them: Carnaby Street, Mary Quant, the Mini Skirt, Mods and Rockers, The Beatles, The Mersey Beat, Hippies, Juke Box Jury, the Mini Cooper, the Moon Landing, Martin Luther King, the Assassination of President Kennedy, Jean Shrimpton, David Bailey, Twiggy, the First Heart Transplant, Woodstock, the Death of Walt Disney, England win World Football Cup, the Sex Revolution, Free Love, and many many more things, not forgetting Russ Sainty and The Nu-Notes, who now have a cult following.

It is early 1960 and Russ and The Nu-Notes get a new manager, whose name is Franklyn Boyd, himself a singer, though definitely not Rock 'n' Roll. He was an important part of the music publishers, Aberbach Music Ltd., situated in Saville Row, London. Frank was also a regular singer with the BBC, and it was because of this that he was able to get us an audition with the Beeb, which thankfully we passed, to be informed that we would be used in the future! Meanwhile, we were still doing all the dance hall gigs for Ron King, with The Dave Clark Five, Chris Farlowe, Rory Storm and others supporting us. And I have to say, it was a big surprise that some years later both Dave Clark and Chris Farlowe should have such massive hit records. But not taking anything away from them, they hit the jackpot, and good luck to them! It was whilst doing a regular dance hall booking at Romford, that a Mr Eddy Green, from Dunstable in Bedfordshire, came to see us perform. I remember that Saturday night very well. Our support was Rory Storm and The Hurricanes, and it was a night that we really had the place rockin'! He approached us following the show, and asked if we would be interested in doing the opening night of his new venue, called the California Pool Ballroom in Dunstable,

A photo taken in Rhet Stoller's front room, early 1960, showing from the left: Rhet Stoller, Bernie Martin, Roy Toft, Russ Sainty and Mel Miller.

Beds. He said he was very impressed with our performance and would be prepared to pay us £25 for that opening night, the 12th March. Blimey; we all looked at each other in surprise, as this was almost twice the amount we were getting paid by Ron King. We agreed to do the show and shook hands on the deal, which was later confirmed by Mr Green in writing. (Little did we know the significance of this booking and what it would lead to).

We continued doing bookings at American air bases, dance hall gigs, the prestigious Pigalle Club at Piccadilly, and equally so the Café de Paris at Leicester Square. I then got a phone call from our new manager, who up till now hadn't done a lot. He gave me a date, time and place for what he called a very important audition, and we must be at our very best. We all decided to go to Cecil Gee's menswear in Charing Cross Road and kitted ourselves out with smart grey trousers and royal blue jackets, and as a personal touch I bought myself a lovely pair of black and white shoes. Time came for us to do the audition, and things went as well as we could hope for. We then sit and wait for some reaction from a panel of about four people. After ten minutes or so Franklyn comes over and tells us the result. "Boys, you have just landed yourselves a summer season at the new Butlins in Bognor Regis." He said, "It's a short season, starting the first week in July through until the end of September, and I've managed to get you £150 per week, £30 each, but out of this you will have to find your own accommodation and food as they won't allow you to live on the Camp." Mmm, we were all excited, but a bit concerned at not living on site. For me, this will require some serious thinking. If I want to stay with The Nu-Notes and do a summer season, it means that I will have to quit my job. Oh dear, the reality of this is just beginning to sink in. I've done my apprenticeship, I have my RHS junior certificate, I'm now reaping the rewards of all my studies as propagator for the Leyton Borough Council Nursery, and above all I do love my job. I tell Franklyn Boyd that I need a few days to make my decision, and it's not going to be easy. The boys are quite happy to wait, as they too need to think about this; after all, this is a big jump to make, and would make us all professional rather than semi-pro entertainers. Well, for me this was a very worrying time. My head was doing somersaults, and I couldn't sleep properly. Oh, what the hell should I do? I speak to my parents and all my work mates, and I'm getting the message that I should take a plunge and go for it. If I fail, I can always come back to horticulture. I made an appointment to speak to my boss, Mr Mason, and he was so understanding and said to me, "Alfred, this is no surprise to me and I half expected this might happen. We shall miss you very much and I wish you every success as a singer." I thanked him for all his tremendous support

The California Pool Ballroom as it was when we first saw it in March 1960. *Photo courtesy of Diane Ilka*

throughout my time at the nursery and then we arranged a date for me to leave. This was indeed a very sad time for me, but inside was a burning desire to become a Rock 'n' Roll star. On a happy note, Mum had been home from hospital a few months by now and was looking great. I had not seen her looking so well. However, had she still been ill, I don't think I would have agreed to go away for a summer season.

Well, Butlins is a little way off yet, and we still have plenty of bookings to fulfill, including Saturday March 12th at the California Pool Ballroom. We load up Mr Stoller's van and set off for Dunstable. We pick up the brand new Ml Motorway en route, which I have to say was almost empty, unlike today when it is more like a car park. As we drove towards the Dunstable Downs, one of the boys shouted, "that's it up there, it looks like a big place." We pulled up in front of this very big building and just stared. Wow! This looks a bit special, I was thinking. We start taking our equipment inside and discover a huge ballroom, bigger than anything I'd ever seen before. We met

Having entered the building to set up on the small stage, we are all blown away by the size of this magnificent ballroom, and a little intimidated!! *Photo courtesy of Diane Ilka*

Dennis, the manager, who told us to set up at the far end, on the small stage. He said, "Ray Miller Orchestra will be on the big stage, with guest singer Ronnie Carroll, and the boss's daughter Edwina, who is also a singer." He also told us that the Lord Mayor of Luton would be doing the official opening. I thought, blimey, this is gonna be some night, and sure enough that's the way it turned out, with bus loads of people being dropped off, and hundreds of private cars and taxis. In no time at all, the place was heaving. In all around 800 people were in by 8.15pm, and the place was buzzing with excitement and anticipation. The only thing this place didn't have was a dressing room. We had to get changed in the kitchens, but that didn't bother us one little bit; this place was the best booking we had had so far.

So what do I recall of that opening night in terms of performance by us and indeed The Ray Miller Orchestra and guest singer Ronnie Carroll? Well, let me take you through the evening, as I remember it, with the odd calculated guess thrown in, it was of course 50 years ago! Having been told by Little Dennis that we were to set up our equipment on the small stage at the far end of the ballroom, it was after only ten minutes or so that he returned, telling us how the evening programme would run, and it was quite clear that he, like ourselves, was feeling a mixture of excitement, apprehension and in his case, outright fear, that something might go wrong! It would be The

Ray Miller Orchestra to open up proceedings at 8pm and play until 9pm, followed by Russ Sainty and The Nu-Notes until 9.45pm. I believe Ray Miller then took over and played a few numbers, after which at around 10pm, guest singer Ronnie Carroll was brought on until around 10.45pm. However, it was amongst all of us musicians doing our bit that Mr Green delivered a short speech and introduced the Lord Mayor of Luton onto the stage, who in turn gave a short speech, officially opening the Ballroom. The Ray Miller Orchestra then played a few more numbers, after which at around 11pm myself and The Nu-Notes would have done the last hour, taking us up to closing time of 12 midnight. I can't recall any problems with the performances in the Ballroom. I believe it would be correct to say that everything went like a dream. What does stand out in my memory is that it really was very exciting, with the audience crowding around the stage at least ten deep, Cheering, screaming and applauding every song we performed. I recall us all being completely "shattered" at the close of our last number, which I believe was

Russ and The Nu-Notes giving everything on opening night at the 'Cali', March 12th 1960.

a gentle ballad. I have in fact prepared a list of many of the songs which we performed on that very special opening night, and can tell you that the number which went down best for us that wonderful evening was an Elvis Presley song called "Wear my Ring Around your Neck", a fast pulsating rocker, which shook The Brand New Cali to its foundations. Of course, as I've mentioned already, the atmosphere in the Ballroom that night was just fantastic, and all those apprehensions and worries by Little Dennis, and I guess the entire Green family, about things going wrong were completely blown away; the opening night was a great success. I didn't get a chance to speak to any member of The Ray Miller Orchestra that night; we were all far too busy and focused on the job. I did however chat to Ronnie Carroll, who at this time was in the prime of his career, and he told me how he had enjoyed the night, after which he agreed to have photos taken with myself and The Nu-Notes. The Boys and I then chatted and signed autographs for the dozens of people who waited around after our last number. It was indeed the beginning of what developed into great friendships and a massive fan base with, in particular, the people of the surrounding areas of Bedfordshire, Buckinghamshire, Hertfordshire and Oxfordshire.

Opening night at the 'Cali', Russ and the Boys have a quick photo call with Ronnie Carroll at the end of what was a truly great evening.

The upstairs bar, situated above and just behind the main stage, where we would enjoy a lager and lime between sets. *Photo courtesy of Diane Ilka*

At the end of what had been a fantastic night for everyone, Mr Green, the boss, took us upstairs for a drink with his family, and his face was glowing with delight and relief that this opening night had been a total success all round. He then spoke to Mr Stoller and immediately booked us for every spare Friday and Saturday we had, which included all dates up to and including Christmas, following our season at Butlins. This was fantastic, and I was feeling more and more that my decision to go fully professional was the right one, but only time would tell.

Feeling rather "cock a hoop", happy and excited about what was a fabulous opening night, we start to load up Mr Stoller's Bedford van, then set off for the new M1 Motorway, which in 1960 only went as far as the Bushey-Watford area, where it suddenly came to an end. However, the consolation was, as you came off the motorway, just a few hundred metres down the road was the famous transport cafe called the Busy Bee, and believe me, it was always very busy. We would pull in and have a pit stop, usually order a large mug of tea, with double egg and chips, with a slice of bread and butter. Unfortunately for me, I like my egg yolks well cooked, but no luck at the Busy Bee, oh no, they were always like jelly and under cooked! However, this was all part of the fun and prepared us for unloading the van at 13, Glaserton Road, Stamford Hill, the Stoller home, and then to re-load Mr Stoller's boxes of kippers. Oh happy days, it only seems like yesterday!

RUSS SAINTY and THE NU-NOTES SONG LIST
OPENING NIGHT AT THE 'CALI' 12 MARCH 1960

The following are some of the songs that myself and members of The Nu-Notes can recall performing on opening night, but in no particular order:

Hound Dog
Too Much
Loving You
Teddy Bear
A Fool Such As I
Blue Suede Shoes
I Need Your Love Tonight
Wear My Ring Around Your Neck
All Elvis Presley Hits

One of These Mornings
I Believe what You Say
It's Late
Poor Little Fool
I Gotta Feeling
Never Be Anyone Else But You
All Ricky Nelson Hits

Move It
Travelling Light
Living Doll
All Cliff Richard Hits

Johnny B Goode
Chuck Berry Hit

I'm in Love Again
Fats Domino Hit

Queen of the Hop
Bobby Darin Hit

Be Bop ALula
Gene Vincent Hit

Teenager in Love
Only Sixteen
Both Craig Douglas Hits

Only Make Believe
Conway Twitty Hit

Why
Tony Newley Hit

Caravan
Tico Tico
Standard Instrumentals

Dream Lover
Bobby Darin Hit

Oh Boy
It Doesn't Matter Any More
Both Buddy Holly Hits

All I Have to do is Dream
Wake Up Little Susie
Both Everly Brothers Hits

A Whole Lotta Shakin'
Jerry Lee Lewis Hit

Here Comes Summer
Jerry Keller Hit

May 1960, Russ and the Boys still rockin' at the 'Cali'.

Following that memorable Saturday night at the 'Cali', on Dunstable Downs, we have Sunday off, but are back rehearsing on Monday evening, thanks to the caretaker of a small Jewish School at Stamford Hill, North London, where we rehearsed on a regular basis. Naturally we talked about our great opening night in Dunstable, and for one reason or another we all felt that this marked a turning point in our Rock 'n' Roll careers! It was quite clear from that very first night, that our bookings at the 'Cali' were special. Apart from the size of the place, there were other magic ingredients evident on the very first night. Let's be honest, it was not the most plush of ballrooms, but it was comfortable and friendly, with a warm ambience; it also had two stages, which was a great help with continuity and non stop music. And I think the fact that this place was out of town was an advantage; it was somewhere to travel to, which made the evening that little bit more special. As the weeks went by, it

was clear to see friendships growing weekly. It was home from home; safe but with a great night's entertainment thrown in, not forgetting that Eddy Green factor! With The Ray Miller Orchestra and ourselves working together sometimes twice weekly, this did give a greater variation in the music played, which I believe in the beginning was another of those ingredients which made the 'Cali' special. You would have thought that The Ray Miller Orchestra and ourselves would have been all "buddie buddie", but in truth we never got to know each other that well. For one thing, when they were on stage performing, we would be upstairs in the bar having a lager and lime, and this situation would be in reverse as soon as they came off and we took the

May 1960, Russ and The Nu-Notes keep rockin' down on the small stage at the 'Cali'.

stage. I guess another reason was the length of the Ballroom. It would have been easier for us to say hello by semaphore with a couple of flags! We were however all good friends, after all this was the 'Cali'. This combination of Rock 'n' Roll (Beat Group) with the orchestra big band sound was extremely successful for the first couple of years, but eventually this had to give way, and from around 1963 the format changed. Out went the orchestra big band sound, and in came total Rock 'n' Roll beat group sounds, with all the best of British and later the best of the United States taking to the stage at the 'Cali'. Thankfully, Russ Sainty and The Nu-Notes continued to be booked on a regular basis.

A rare post card give-away photo, especially taken for our summer season at Butlins, Bognor Regis, June 1960.

Chapter Six

SUMMER LOVIN'
AT BUTLINS

O h, how my memory is racing away, but for all that, it's back to Monday evening's rehearsal at Stamford Hill, North London, 14th March 1960. Rehearsals go well, and as the next few weeks go by, we start to make our preparations for our Summer Season at Butlins, Bognor Regis, on the South Coast, and book some accommodation. We decide on the George Inn, situated at the far end of Bognor High Street, so we are all set to go. A week later, having now quit my job and said my farewells, I give my mum a hug and go to the Stollers' house at Stamford Hill. We load the van and set off for Bognor Regis, where first stop is the George Inn to drop off our personal belongings and choose a bed. Following this, we make for Butlins Camp, a mile down the road. The first thing we notice is that workmen are still building some areas of the Camp, it's definitely not finished. However, we meet the head of entertainment, a Mr Haywood, who directs us upstairs to a really massive ballroom, called The Rock and Calypso Ballroom, Wow! This is nice, I'm thinking, but very big.

So we set up and start to make ourselves at home. Mr Haywood tells us that we are to play a two-hour set each afternoon, and a three-hour set each evening for six days a week, each week throughout the season. Bloody hell, is he joking or what? We only have enough material for about one and a half hours! Five hours a day is a lot of singing, to put it mildly. This is going to be tough. We have a walk around the Camp, and it's massive, and then we find another ballroom, which is much bigger than ours, and we are told that the famous Eric Winstone Orchestra will play here, with guest duo The Brook Brothers, who had recently been in the Hit Parade with a song called "War Paint". The next day is opening day, and for Russ Sainty and The Nu-Notes, this is IT! Now, I have to say it was bloody hard going for a few days, but we were learning new songs and instrumentals, and scraping by. Even though we played the same songs two or three times a day, we just didn't

A photo taken in February 2008, showing the pub/hotel, in which Russ Sainty and The Nu-Notes stayed for bed and breakfast, when doing that first summer season away from home at Butlins Bognor Regis, namely The George Inn. Though it now looks to have had a name change to The Unicorn.

have a choice. Our big problem was food; we weren't getting enough of it and, to make matters worse, the George Inn expected us in by 11pm, which was ridiculous. I remember Barry Stoller climbing two storeys up a drainpipe and clambering through the window at about 2am, only to be caught by the owner. Ha ha, we all giggled our socks off! This was no good, so we had to get out of the George Inn. We find a big caravan on a site quite near to the Camp, and decide to rent it immediately and move in that same night. Wowie! This is more like it; we can now do our own thing and eat when we want. Well, I have to tell you, this was the beginning of a whole lotta fun, as you might guess.

Now, as group leader and the eldest by far, I took it upon myself to have a sort of fatherly chat with the Boys. Amongst a lot of advice, I did stress that we would need to work hard at our new careers in a professional way, and this meant no girls! Well, at least no serious relationships, because I felt this would hold back our chances of becoming a big success. At this time, it was considered the kiss of death for a pop singer or group to have a girlfriend, so I made a strong point that this must not happen; it's strictly one-night stands only. Well, I have to tell you dear reader, these are comments I nearly regretted for the rest of my life. You can guess what's coming next. Having been at Butlins for about a week, following an afternoon show a group of young, beautiful, female Redcoats drifted up the stairs and sat down at the rear of our ballroom. We then drifted towards them and started to make silly comments, I personally picking on a very attractive blonde girl, with a cracking pair of legs, who told me her name was Ann. Well, we finished up asking the girls to try and get us some Butlins food, and we would meet up later that night. Oh blimey, she is nice, I was thinking to myself. What's going on here, am I in for a one-night stand already? Or maybe not, but I really fancy her. We did all meet up later, but Butlins law did not allow its staff to chat or fraternise together, which made life difficult at times. Amazingly enough, each of us apart from Barry Stoller had chosen a different girl from the group,

Photo showing Ann Graham, a 17-year-old Butlins Red Coat, who became Russ Sainty's girlfriend and whom Russ married in 1965.

which worked out perfectly, but we didn't worry about Barry Stoller, because to be honest, at this time, he was still a spoilt Mummy's and Daddy's boy and would have to toughen up a bit. He really was a wimp, threatening to pack up and go home every other day. However, I have to tell you that we now really started to have fun, meeting the four girls after work had finished each night at about 11pm, and then all moving off camp and round to our caravan. We would then have a massive cook up, with Radio Luxemburg blasting out all the hits of the day; this was the best time ever, believe me! Some nights we would not even get to sleep at all, and the girls had to be back on duty at 7.30am the next morning. Crazy or what? Yes, perhaps it was, but we were all young, and this was fun and freedom, something we had never experienced before, and for Mel, Roy and Bernie,

A very rare picture of Russ Sainty performing on stage at Butlins, Bognor Regis, summer 1960.

this was their first girlfriend. And, though I was the eldest by far at age 24 years, Ann was only my second girlfriend – a mere 17 years old. Things would continue in the same way for another week, then we decided to ditch the caravan and rent a really nice flat in Bognor High Street. This meant we all had a proper bed and decent cooking facilities. Meanwhile, on 14th July, Ann had become a woman, as it was her 18th birthday. So much had happened in a couple of weeks, it felt like we had been away for months. On our day off, I would drive us all back home in my new black Ford Thames van, which I had bought earlier in the year. My first little van, painted in two tones of green, was sold to one of my old army mates, Teddy

Winkley, a twin brother to Barney, who both lived at The Elephant and Castle. Having by now been at Butlins about a month, we were doing our shows on automatic, as the whole thing was a bit impersonal, I guess because the ballroom was so big. However, we were doing very well and management were happy. I was by now crazy about Ann, and actually wrote on one of my promotion photos, "Ann, one day you are the girl I'm going to marry." That's the sort of state I was in. Yes, I know what you must be thinking – that fatherly chat I had with the Boys about girls and no serious relationships. Oh dear, I'm lost for words.

right A photo taken by a guest at Butlins showing Russ with Rhet Stoller, Mel Miller and Roy Toft; can't think where Bernie Martin was.

below Butlins 1960, Russ Sainty doing his duty as a judge for the weekly competition, "Miss She".

Our manager, Franklyn Boyd, made contact with us and said that we must be on our very best form for our evening session, because he was bringing down from London a very important person who could get us a record contract. His name was Bunny Lewis, the man behind all the hits, and manager of such people as Craig Douglas ("Only Sixteen"), The Mudlarks ("Lollypop"), The Avons ("Seven Little Girls, Sitting in the Back Seat!") and broadcaster Alan Freeman. Well, that evening, sure enough, Franklyn and Bunny sat watching us perform, and, during our break, Bunny told us that he would send down a demo record of a song called "Happy Go Lucky Me", and told us to rehearse the song, ready to record on our next day off. The following week, we are told to make our way to a studio in Portland Place, just across the road from BBC's Broadcasting House. I believe the studio was called ITC Recording Studios. Well, I have to say, this being our first time in a recording studio it was all a bit daunting, and nothing remotely like the workings of studios today. We must have done about 25 takes before Bunny was happy, and even then he was still not sure. The truth is, this song was not suitable for myself and the group and it would never sound right. We needed a good pop song, and this was just not the one.

We also recorded a song composed by Barry Stoller called "Standing Around", which was to be the B side of the record. Our recording came out on the new Top Rank label, but we had massive competition, with the American version by composer Paul Williams, also other English versions by George Formby, ha ha, and Frank Ifield, and it just killed off any chances of the song becoming a hit! Whilst all this was going on, Bunny Lewis wants The Nu-Notes to record an instrumental which was a big hit in America for a group called The Ventures, and the tune, "Walk Don't Run ". By now, Dick Row, who was in charge at Top Rank Records, has moved to Decca Records, so off to Decca Studios we go to cut this instrumental. Well, I have to tell you for some reason known only to him, Barry Stoller decided to play the number in a different key from the original American hit, and it proved to be a disaster. Barry could not play the whole number through without making mistakes, so it was decided that they would use the first chorus, which he had played correctly, and somehow re-record this section, so that the same bit was actually played twice to make the recording complete – a little secret that until now nobody ever knew about. Of course, these days, recording studios can do the most incredible things, even to put an out of tune singer back in tune. I think the general public would be shocked at how a completed record is made in this modern age. On the B side would be a number composed by Barry called "All Rhet", and the reason for that name was that Bunny Lewis and our manager Franklyn had decided in their wisdom that Barry, as lead guitarist, should change his name to Rhet Stoller, and the record went out as performed by The Rhet Stoller Group. This was all a bit confusing as we were still Russ Sainty and The Nu-Notes, but we were told that the reason for a name change was a marketing ploy.

I cannot begin to explain how exciting it was, to be walking along the Bognor sea front with a portable radio tuned in to Radio Luxemburg, when suddenly one of our records would come blasting out, it was such a thrill. In those days, most young people would tune in to Radio Luxemburg, because all the record companies were paying to have their new releases played on what was a commercial station, funded by advertising. It had a sort of magic about it, fading in and fading out. We would try to place the portable in a position to receive the best signal, but this would be constantly changing, and it seemed you would always lose the signal at the most important moments, but for all that we all loved Radio Luxemburg, great stuff!

We next get a call from Franklyn, who informs us, you are booked for your first BBC broadcast. You will be on the Beeb's top pop show, "Saturday Club", compered by Brian Matthew and produced by Jimmy Grant! Well, little did we know it then, but this first booking was to lead to several hundred more over the next few years, but I'll come to that later. We are now beginning to realize that things happen fast in show biz, and, though we are all tired from the five hours a day performing and now the extra trips to London, we know that we have to take things as they come and stop moaning about tiredness – which was happening with certain members, Barry! This summer has gone better than ever we had imagined, and before long we will hit the big time, I feel sure. Having said that, both mine and Rhet's singles have flopped, but they have exposed us via Radio Luxemburg to the whole of the U.K. and Europe, so that's got to be good!

With about a month left to complete our season at Butlins, both Rhet and myself receive from Bunny Lewis demo records of numbers to learn and arrange for our next record release. My numbers are "Too Shy" and "Race with the Devil", and Barry's (Rhet) are "Chariot" and "Night Theme". We both get stuck into learning and arranging the numbers and I must admit that Barry found some lovely little guitar parts for "Too Shy", but to be honest I didn't think that the song was strong enough to be a hit. I did however think that "Chariot" was a great number and might well be a hit for the Boys.

The season at Butlins finally comes to an end, and Mr Stoller comes down with his big van to collect all our equipment and take the Boys back home to Stamford Hill, North London. As for me, well, I was in love, and Ann had

September 1960, Ann Graham and Russ in the back garden of Russ's home, following a great summer season at Butlins Bognor Regis.

spoken to her parents asking if she could go to London with me and get herself a flat. They were quite happy with that, but first Ann would come back to Leyton with me and meet my parents and sister. We arrived home and I took Ann into the house to meet everyone, but I recall the atmosphere was a bit frosty at first, which I didn't understand because they didn't even know her. However, it wasn't going to change anything between us but did make me feel on edge, slightly embarrassed and disappointed. Anyway, after a few days, Ann went to stay with other friends for a while, until getting a job and her own flat, which thereafter made life better for us.

Having had a decent break, we now get into the Decca recording studios, where to our surprise we meet The Michael Sams Singers (Mike and Three Women), who would be doing all the vocal backing voices on both my songs, great stuff! I'm really chuffed about that. Well, we decide to record "Too Shy" first, and that goes well and is in the can after about three takes. We then try "Race With The Devil", which is quite fast, and was sounding good, but unlike today we were all partitioned off into separate boxes, in order that they can control the sound of each individual, and in those days none of us had the luxury of earphones (cans as they are known), which made it very hard to hear what each of us was doing. This had quite an effect on poor Bernie on drums, who struggled to keep in time with the rest of the group, and for any 1960s cult followers who may have the record, if you listen carefully you will notice Bernie does go out of time. Another little secret exposed (hope I don't get put in the tower!). With the record completed, it's just a case of waiting for a release date. In the meantime, we are back at the California Pool Ballroom every weekend, and we are also back doing a few dance hall gigs for Ron King. Then, out of the blue, the group are called in to record their two numbers "Chariot" and

MEET THE BOY WHO IS TIPPED FOR THE TOP WITH HIS SECOND DISC

'Shy' Mr. Sainty knows he can do it

"I'D rather dig the music . . . than dig the soil," says a new young man of discdom who has quite cheerfully thrown up a job for which he served a long apprenticeship in order to concentrate on making a success as a singer.

Russ Sainty's the young man—and his Decca disc of "Too Shy" gets one of this week's tips for the Hit Parade.

The name may be new to you but this is not Russ's first record. He made one for Top Rank with his instrumental group The Nu-Notes; a version of "Happy Go Lucky Me" which has sold quite steadily if not spectacularly.

But with "Too Shy" Sainty could hit the jackpot. And if he doesn't do it with this one he's quite convinced he'll do it with the next one . . . or the next.

"I'm determined to become a fully fledged entertainer," says Russ, "a singer who is also a pretty complete performer."

Natural

Russ was born Alfred Charles Sainty and has lived most of his 21 years in Leyton, Essex. His father is a tree pruner for the local Borough Council and it seemed the natural thing to do for Russ to go into some kind of horticultural work.

For seven years he served his apprenticeship as a seed propagator, learning the ticklish science of cultivating seeds. And he worked for a full year at this job after his apprenticeship was over.

Then the music bug got under his skin and he began drifting towards Soho and the 2 I's Coffee Bar, where he first started sing-

ing in public. Then he teamed up with the Nu-Notes and the act developed around a succession of dates in cinemas and American forces camps.

Soon he decided he had to choose between being a man of the soil or a man of music. And music has won.

"I don't miss gardening," Russ admits. "In fact I'm rather glad to get away from it. I'm not keeping it up even as a hobby.

Not ambitious

"Generally speaking I'm not an extravagant character and I haven't given any thought about what I'd do if the big money comes along.

"See the world? No, I'm not ambitious in that sort of way. I think I'd invest money in some kind of business. You know, stack it away and let it work for me.

"My main thoughts are all on getting ahead in show business and the main target so far as I'm concerned is films. I want to get into pictures if I can."

At the moment Russ is winding up a season at Butlin's Holiday Camp in Bognor Regis. He finishes there on September 16 and has some one-night stands and radio dates lined up.

"Butlins has been marvellous experience for me, but it's been tough work," says Russ, "I've been singing with the group for five hours every day, which is a bit of a strain. But I'm proud to say the audiences have been reacting wonderfully. Real mixed audiences of all ages, too."

D. N.

September 1960

"Night Theme". I was able to play a very fast tambourine on "Chariot", and the Harry Robinson Orchestra put some very nice string sounds onto "Night Theme". We all felt that this record was good and had high hopes of a hit, but once again this would be marketed under the name Rhet Stoller Group.

It's October and, with our records about to be released, we are told by Franklyn Boyd that we are going on a big package tour of the U.K. Marvellous, I thought, and asked Frank, "Are we going on our own?" To which he just giggled and said, "Not on your Nellie, let me put you in the picture." He then named the personnel, Craig Douglas, top of the bill, ("Only Sixteen", "Pretty Blue Eyes") Ricky Valance ("Tell Laura I Love Her"), The Avons ("Seven Little Girls, Sitting In The Back Seat"), The Mudlarks ("Lollypop"), Mike Preston ("I'm Mr Blue"), Russ Sainty ("Too Shy"), and The Rhet Stoller Group ("Chariot"), with Alan (Fluff) Freeman as compere. He then explained that The Nu-Notes (Rhet Stoller Group) would accompany all the acts and do their own spot. Blimey, I was thinking, they have got their work cut out, better give Barry a headache tablet. My only memory of rehearsals was that of Ricky Valance, a Welsh lad with a number one hit, but he was so cocky and nasty with it, telling everyone that he should be top of the bill, he went on and on griping and moaning, so much so that I had a big row with him and had to put him straight. However, the Boys would get their own back at a later date.

MAKING his Decca debut is British boy Russ Sainty with a polished up-tempo song. "Too Shy." There is a girl group behind him as well as the instrumental backing of the Nu-Notes team.

Sainty should find himself in the hit parade as a result of this half. The melody is easy to catch and the idea is neat. Sainty's voice fits the present day mood.

"Race With The Devil" is quicker to fit the title of the number. The Nu-Notes' backing here is very good indeed, but I did not care for the gimmicky "bogey man" laugh which seemed quite unnecessary.

September 1960

With all rehearsals completed, the Boys were quite relieved, but had a lot on their plate. However, this would be a fantastic experience for them, playing for so many different top performers. I can't recall where the tour began, but I do recall it being a great first night, making everyone involved happy to say the least! As for Ricky Valance, the Boys did get their own back for his previous antics and cocky-ness. On the very last night of the tour, whilst about to sing his number one hit song, "Tell Laura I Love Her", The Nu-Notes played his backing a tone higher than it should have been, causing Ricky to really struggle with all the top notes. Oh, how satisfying it was to see Mr Cocky in trouble, and he could do nothing about it. Revenge is sometimes very sweet!

★ On stage and film ★
Craig Douglas is a real bill-topper

THE Craig Douglas package opened a short tour at the Savoy, Paddington, where the audience got good value for their money. Craig justified his bill-topping status with the most polished and professional performance that I have seen from a teenage star.

Mixing in some fast-moving oldies with his own songs, he moved about the stage with ease and confidence; he has enough ability as a performer not to have to rely on hit records for continued success.

Al Saxon sang, played trumpet, banjo and piano—an exciting and entertaining act that would be more appreciated at the Pigalle than in Paddington, and probably even more so in Las Vegas.

The Mudlarks were good both visually and vocally—a slick and imaginative act that is obviously well rehearsed.

Ricky Valance was mostly inaudible because he held his microphone too close and he has much to learn about "selling" both himself and his songs.

His singing of "Tell Laura," however, evoked loud squeals of delight from the girls.

Russ Sainty was well received and was at his best with the tough, hard hitting "Race with the Devil." Rhet Stoller's group worked hard on stage providing backings for all the singers as well as having a spot to themselves.

As compere, Alan Freeman behaved with such ease and confidence that if the roof had fallen in. I'm sure he wouldn't have batted an eyelid. He'd have just told the audience to put it back up again.

DON'T BELIEVE HIM DONNA, Russ Sainty (Decca 45 F 11270).—Apparently Mr. Sainty has changed his style of singing, alarming his recording manager by the noise he produced. He sings in much the same way as Brando talks, with lots of grunts and hesitations and stuttering, but he claims to feel "uninhibited." I like the result, and also like the way he sings "Donner" instead of "Donna." Very English.

Russ Sainty (21) has been appearing at a Bognor Regis holiday camp this summer. Got his break from singing at the Soho Two I's Coffee Bar. Born Alfred Charles Sainty in Leyton, Essex. Previous job: seed propagation. First disc: "Too Shy" (Decca F11270).

Rus...

Vocal tea...

Don't B...

(De
RUSS S... again... idea to hel... **Don't Beli**... While R... plea to t... vocal team... telling Do... teeth!

This on... make us a... owing mu... backing.

Latin be... in slick fa... has a lot to...

A story series inspired by some of your favourite songs...

A DISC TO REMEMBER

THIS WEEK
"Too Shy" sung by RUSS SAINTY

Russ sings "Too Shy" on Decca F11270

WHENEVER I hear the strains of that lovely number I remember my first date with the boy I loved ... I remember my new outfit and i should have been happy—but i was shaking with shyness.

DON'T
HIM, I

RUSS S

45-F 11325

RUSS SAINTY

holiday camp at Bognor Regis, Sussex. It led to a series of BBC broadcasts, a tour of one-night stands and a recording contract.

On disc, Russ sings **Don't Believe Him, Donna** (Decca).

RUSS SAINTY

"RUSS FOR US!"—you say!

RUSS SAINTY'S the new singing boy the gals are falling for! How do I know? Well, from the letters you've sent, asking all about him! Russ is twenty-one and London-born—lives with his parents and sister at Leyton. His first singing dates began a year or so ago at the 2 I's Coffee Bar in London's Soho. Then he joined up with guitarist Rhet Stoller's group and started cutting discs.

THE group went down a wow at Butlin's, Bognor, last summer—and they plan a return visit this year. You'll have heard...

Russ Sainty

Li
A
brin
Jazz
broa
Al
over
on
Jazz
Septe
Gu
includ
Masie

October 1960

Chapter Seven

THE MODEL SINGER

It's the 5th of November 1960 and, following our tour, Russ Sainty and The Nu-Notes are back at the 'Cali', and what's more I am about to create my first Cali record. I will perform twenty two consecutive 45-minute sets, the last being on December 9th. As far as The Nu-Notes are concerned, our booking on the 5th November was to be the last under that name, not without a bit of bad feeling all round.

Throughout my life, I can honestly say I've always been quite modest and humble about anything I've achieved, but right now, at the age of a very young 70+ years, my modesty is going straight out of the window. As this story comes to the end of the year 1960, it is with great pride that, even though I didn't start until 12th March and then had a Summer Season for Butlins, followed by a tour with Craig Douglas and Ricky Valance, I recall managing to complete forty-seven (47) bookings at the California Ballroom, which equates to ninety-four (94) separate 45-minute sets, and yes, on most occasions we topped the bill. I hope you will forgive me, but I think these statistics are enough to make anyone feel proud. What will next year bring, you may wonder? Well stick with me, because I'm about to let the "cat out of the bag".

The Promotion Department

of the

DECCA RECORD COMPANY

cordially invite

Rus Sainty

to their CHRISTMAS PARTY at

23 Hanover Court W.1

on Wednesday December 21st

from 3 o'clock till 8

R.S.V.P.

left It's Christmas 1960 at the 'Cali' and Russ sings a love song to his girlfriend Ann Graham at the end a wonderful evening.

An invitation to Decca Recording Company's 1960 Christmas party.

Carnaby Street is fast becoming a world tourist attraction, and London's fair city has a new name – Swinging London. Following the recent Rock 'n' Roll, Pop Music revolution, there is now a young people's fashion revolution about to turn the clothing industry upside down! Exciting new style clothing in never-seen-before colours is creating a wonderful sense of joy, happiness and a good-to-be-young feeling, and what's more, I'm about to become a big part of it – the whole scene – no, not just as a singer but also as a photographic model!

Bookings for the 'Cali' are pouring in. Mr Green has booked us for at least six months ahead, and we have to fit in a ten day tour of Scotland somehow. However, before we can even think of that, we need to get some transport of our own. God Bless Him, we can't expect Rhet's father to drive us around Scotland – he's done more than his share for us and has never taken a penny in expenses and running costs.

Our brand new Commer mini bus parked outside my house in Leyton. Note the large Caribonium factory in the background, year 1961. This was however demolished a few years later.

Meanwhile, we get some good news from our manager Franklyn Boyd, who tells us that our recent instrumental single "Chariot" is at number 26 in The New Musical Express charts! We are all ecstatic and feel that at last this might be our breakthrough on the record scene. Yippee! OK, coming right back to earth, we need to address the subject of transport. We only have one option, and that is for me to trade in my small Ford Thames van as a deposit on a brand new Commer Minibus. I did this on condition that I could use the vehicle as my own, and HP payments would come out of our earnings. The boys were delighted with this arrangement. At last, we are now completely mobile and have the comfort of our own small bus, smashing! We set off for Scotland, and with me the only driver. I know it's going to be hard work. Anyway, we get to Perth and pull into a very large transport cafe car park, one I had been to many years earlier when delivering furniture with my other cousin Denny Stacey, long distance lorry driver. We had something to eat, and did all what one has to do! Then slept the night in the bus. Early the next morning, we went back into the cafe for some breakie, and started talking to a couple of lorry drivers, and they told us what they considered the best route to Elgin, and then on to Lossiemouth, where we had booked bed and breakfast to use as our main base. We thanked the guys and set of on the A93, rather than my own choice, the coast road. Well, it wasn't too long before we started to meet snow, and the road was getting very dodgy indeed. We stopped and I checked the map, only to find that these guys had sent us on the highest road in Great Britain, and on the infamous Devil's Elbow, where we get completely stuck in deep snow. Oh my God, what the hell are we doing here, those lorry drivers have seen us coming, and the laugh is definitely on us idiots! Thankfully, we are full AA members and use the emergency phone box – especially for fools like us? Well, two AA landrovers turned up and, with one pulling and the other one pushing us, we made it over the highest part of the Elbow. The journey onwards was a nightmare, and at times I almost slid off the road, what a way to start a tour. We finally made it to Elgin, where we went straight into a cafe and had a massive "blow out", after which we headed for our digs at Lossie.

The tour itself was nothing special, just a load of small halls, corn exchanges and town halls, within about a 150-mile radius of, to name a few, places like Elgin, Buckie, Keith, Huntley, Forres, Dufftown and many more. The tour was for about 16 days and, believe me, this was some kind of experience! At almost every venue we would have about a dozen bouncers across the front of the stage, and boy, did we need them. The youngsters in these small fishing towns went completely crazy when we were on stage, and were trying to attack us; it was crazy, and to this day I have never experienced anything like it since. They acted like wild animals everywhere we played. Evidently, they were earning big money as fishermen and just got totally pissed whenever a visiting band came to their town. With the tour over, I return via the East Coast road of Scotland, then eventually onto the old A1 and back home to London; remember, there were only limited amounts of motorway at this time!

Having been home now a few days, I get a call from manager Franklyn Boyd, who tells me that I'm about to make a new single with Decca Records, and this time I will be accompanied by a 30-piece orchestra, with The Mike Sams Singers. Great, but I don't think the boys will be too happy. The songs are "Don't Believe Him Donna", A side, and "Your Other Love", the B side. Having learned the two numbers, the day came to go to Decca studios to record them, and I have to tell you, I was nervous. When I walked into the studio and looked around, I could not believe what I was seeing – the huge

Harry Robinson Orchestra, and Mike Sams with his female singers, Wow! and <u>all</u> this for me, a mere Rock 'n' Roll singer. I was both thrilled and scared. Thinking, please God, help me to do well! Remember in those days, you had to sing the song through with the orchestra, and not mess-up. The recording went extremely well. I just could not believe how good my performance was when singing "Donna". It's a far cry from Rock 'n' Roll, and considering I had never had a singing lesson in my life I was indeed proud of what I had done. Franklyn, my manager, also thought it was a bit special and that I had every chance of a hit single.

Well, the record was released and, whilst we were still doing our weekly shows with more regular BBC Broadcasts coming in as well, Frank called me to say he had fixed some TV appearances to help promote the record. I was thrilled to bits – at last some TV, the one thing that's been missing, perhaps now I might have a hit record on my hands. I do television shows at Manchester, Scotland, N.Ireland, Channel Islands and Cardiff. However, I do all these shows alone without The Nu-Notes. Yes, as you can imagine, there were a few long faces, and group morale slumped, even though I assured the Boys that if my record was a success it would benefit us all, but I don't think I ever convinced them, and there were rumblings of discontent for sure. But, for all that, I have to confess my single didn't make it and we had to look to what may come up for our next recording, that's if there would be another chance.

Fortunately, we had plenty of bookings for months ahead, and had a great reputation as one of the best groups in the country, but just could not get the right material to record, it was all so frustrating! As a measure of the respect we had in

A shot of the Boys doing a bit of gardening.

THE RHET STOLLER GROUP **DECCA RECORDING STARS**

The Rhet Stoller Group. Well, that's what Decca Records say, but of course they were also The Nu-Notes. All very confusing.

the business from our fellow groups and booking promoters, we next get a booking to do a big show at the Gaumont Cinema Edmonton, North London, with Cliff and the Shadows – Russ Sainty and The Nu-Notes doing the whole of the first half, about one and a half hours, and Cliff with The Shads did the whole of the second half, and it was a great show. We were able to include quite a bit of comedy into our show, not difficult when you have a bass player like our Mel Miller, who was just a natural when it came to being funny.

I then get a call from Dick Row of Decca Records, asking me to drop everything and get to the studio as soon as possible. I drive to Leyton tube station, jump on a train and get to the studio in about an hour all told. When I walk in, it's empty, but I can see two men in the recording booth where all the machinery is. I walk in and, to my great surprise, standing with Dick Row was Lionel Bart! He said to me, "Hello Russ, you have come a long way since we last met at the 2 i's Coffee Bar, do you remember?" I replied "Yes, I do remember it very well indeed, and looking back, I think I acted a bit stupid." We just laughed about it and he then said to me, "I want you to come out into the studio with me and try this song on the microphone." He sang it over to me, but I was finding it hard to pick up quickly, since in my opinion it was a bit tuneless, but I kept trying. It was called "Big Time", and I sang it as well as I could, considering I had no music at all, not even a piano to accompany me. They both thanked me for rushing up to the studio and I said my goodbyes and got a train back to Leyton. Another chance with Lionel Bart seems to have passed me by. I was angry with myself, but deep down I knew the song was rubbish. As it happens, a month or so later Adam Faith released a single, and guess what was on the A side? Yes it was "Big Time", and I was happy to see that it didn't do very well at all; if I were to be truthful, it was a flop, which made me feel a lot better, believe me.

During this year of 1961 we do our first of several tours of Lincolnshire, usually lasting a couple of weeks, and we would always stay at The Rodney Hotel, owned then by Mrs Haigh. This was pretty central, situated in the small town of Horncastle, and we had some great times up there and always plenty of laughs. Mrs Haigh owned a race horse, which was stabled at the back of the hotel. I asked her if I could ride him out one morning. "Ride him out?" she said. "This is a race horse and he's quite frisky. Have you ever ridden a horse before?" I said to her, "Don't worry, I was once an apprentice jockey for the Queen's trainer!" She replied, "Well if you've ridden the Queen's horses, you can definitely ride mine, yes take him out tomorrow morning." I then arranged this with her stable lad and the next morning took the horse out, riding him all round the town and local road. Yes, I was a bit nervous at first, as it had been a long time since I was at Newmarket riding racehorses. I also remember one night coming back from a show, when we were all starving hungry and the hotel was closed. Mrs Haigh always gave us a key to get in on occasions like this, that's the kind of relationship we had built up. Well, it was decided between us that we would raid the kitchen and see what was in the fridge. Rhet Stoller drew the short straw, so down the stairs he went. Ten minutes later returning with a tin of peaches. Oh dear, is he crazy or what? His excuse was that the fridge was locked. We didn't see this as stealing, more of a giggle; after all, what can you do with a tin of peaches at about 2.00am in the morning?

It's still the year 1961, and we decide Franklyn Boyd, our manager, is not doing enough for us, and we decide to part company. We are now without both a manager and Bunny Lewis, the man who set up all the records we had made up to this point, had lost faith in us as recording artistes following my last flop, "Don't Believe Him Donna". However, I get a phone call from a Michael McGrath, who had plenty of chat, asking me who was in charge of promoting Russ Sainty and The Nu-Notes and saying that he was in a position to help. Well, I thought, I've heard all this crap before, who is this bloke? But he was if nothing else persistent and assured me that what he had in mind would be very good for me personally, and that it would not cost me a penny. As you can imagine, I was very suspicious, but went over to Chelsea to meet him and see what he had in mind. He was very complimentary about my looks, and assured me that I was being wasted. He insisted that with looks like mine I should be doing photographic modelling work! I laughed, as I had never ever thought myself any kind of model. He then told me his plans, and

A rare early photo of Russ, taken during a working studio session.

again assured me there were no costs for his help. He said, "I want you to be photographed in the very latest fashions from Carnaby Street, specifically for a Mr John Stephen," who owned one of the very first clothes shops to open in The Street. OK, I agreed, and was getting quite excited about this, as I would get myself seen in all magazines, girlie books and various newspapers!

My first day comes and we meet for a shoot down by the River Thames. I'm dressed in all the latest gear and Fred our photographer tells me I'm doing really well, "a natural", he said. Well, I continued doing this for about a year on and off, and sure enough, I was getting all the publicity he had promised me. Not only that, I had now got myself a portfolio together and was with a modelling agency called Pamela Maxfield, who suggested I do the rounds of all the London photographers, showing myself and my portfolio

overleaf A collection of shots taken during 1961, in some of which I am modelling the great new style clothes by John Stephen of Carnaby Street, "Swinging London".

64

RUSS SAINTY

RECORDING STAR OF
"SATURDAY CLUB" & "EASY BEAT"
HIS MASTER'S VOICE RECORDS

RECORDING STAR OF
"SATURDAY CLUB" & "EASY BEAT"

RUSS SAINTY

65

of up-to-date photos. Yes, it was hard work, walking around London, but it paid off, and before long I was making good money from my work, and of course still doing my shows with The Nu-Notes. I auditioned for several TV adverts and soon landed myself a plum job. I was to play the lead role in a television advert for Worthington E, a beer ad. It was filmed over two days, one at Crystal Palace outdoors, and the other in a studio at Shepherds Bush, where we did the entire close up shots of me drinking. Some drink! The producer was after a close up of me taking a big drink, in fact about half a glass, and by the time I had done this about ten times I was feeling very very happy! And talking rubbish. However, he insisted I keep doing just one more shot, until I fell off of the stool! No joking, I was completely drunk. I now realise why they did the close up shot last. Well, I don't recall too much about the next few hours; everyone had left the studio by the time I had come round, except the night security, who phoned my parents to let them know where I was and why I was still there. I was unable to drive home to Leyton, so decided to get a very late tube train and got home finally about 1.30am. The next morning I felt lousy, with a pounding head, but made my way back to Shepherds Bush and picked up my car. All in all, it was quite an experience.

The advert was on TV for a long time, six months or more perhaps, and each time it was on, I made a bit more money, not bad eh? I did get another very nice photographic job. It was for Kensitas cigarettes, and involved myself and a few others travelling to the Spanish Sierra Nevada mountains, where shots of us skiing were required; the whole thing took a week to do. The result was that I was on the big poster hoardings around the country for the next six months or so, not bad considering I've never smoked in my life. I did lots more jobs, far too many to mention, and to think that this all came out of a phone call from Michael McGrath, a guy that came into my life completely out of the blue, and a year or so later disappeared just as quickly! Life can be so strange.

Now up to this point I've tried to be as accurate as possible with regard to the year, the month, the week and sometimes the day of events and happenings in this, the story of my life, but with regard to the BBC it's almost impossible to do this, and this is the reason why; between 1960 and 1966, the amount of broadcasts I did with and without The Nu-Notes totals many hundreds, exactly how many, I'm just not sure, but let's put it this way, you would have to search very very hard to find a pop group such as we were, who did more broadcasts, some recorded and some live on air, than we did, in fact I can't name one. As Russ Sainty and The Nu-Notes, producers knew that when they booked us they didn't need to worry, firstly about us arriving and being set up on time, but perhaps more importantly, they didn't have to worry about our performance. They knew we always delivered the goods, and sometimes at very short notice. We were fortunate enough to have our own thirteen-week series on two occasions, one called "Side by Side" with Lorne Gibson, and compered by Dis Dissley, the other, I just can't recall its title, but I do remember that the producer was Cyril Drake, a really charming

Roy Toft, Russ Sainty and Mel Miller in harmony at the 'Cali', 1961.

man, and each week we would feature the songs of all the big names in pop. Elvis P., The Everlys, Cliff R., Buddy Holly, Bobby Vee and many many more. One of our favourites was "Easy Beat", recorded live on Wednesday at The Playhouse Theatre and broadcast on Sunday morning. On this show we performed with some great names, Kenny Ball's Jazz Band, Clinton Ford, The Springfields, Dusty singing solo, The Rolling Stones and just about anyone who was anyone. We even worked with Vera Lynn on a live recorded show from the Paris Studios Lower Regent Street; it was called "Twenties to the Twist", but I have to say I was very disappointed with her behaviour. Whilst we were rehearsing our numbers, she sat smack bang in front of us, and then put her fingers in her ears, very rude and unprofessional. In 1963 we were guests of The Beatles on a couple of occasions, their programme being "Pop

Go the Beatles". No, we didn't meet up with The Beatles, though I very much would like to have done. Programmes like this and let's say "Saturday Club" would record all the artistes and groups individually and then they would all be linked together by let's say Brian Matthew, as in the case of "Sat. Club". Whereas, with shows like "Easy Beat", we had an audience and the show would be live and recorded to be put out at a later date, and on this kind of show you would meet up with all the other acts.

I was also lucky enough to do many dozens of shows; both live and recorded, with the BBC, singing as Russ Sainty backed by professional studio musicians. This would involve me getting sheet music and full arrangements written up for the guys to play, and this could be different for each show – however, the considerable cost of providing this written music fell upon the publisher of the music, and they would be happy to pay all costs in order to get their song played and exposed via myself and the Beeb, that's the way it worked. It was of course a tremendous thrill for me every time I did a show with say six, eight and sometimes ten brilliant top musicians, such as Don Lusher (trombone), Kenny Clare (drums), Arthur Greenslade (piano), Rex Morris (tenor sax), Tommy Sanderson (piano), Vick Flick (guitar), Bert Weedon (guitar), Johnny Arthey (piano), Harry Stoneham (keyboards), and so many more!

Of all the dozens of solo shows I did, I must mention a couple – the first from London's Ideal Home Exhibition at Olympia, where the BBC, year after year, did a daily midday show live, which was always great fun to do. The other one was even more memorable, and I was very proud to do it. Once a year the Beeb would present a live pop concert from The Royal Albert Hall, and I was lucky enough to do the show, accompanied by The Bob Miller Band. I remember it very well indeed for more reasons than one. The atmosphere back stage was electric, and I was in the company of Jimmy Grant producer, and his secretary Francis Line. We had a few drinks and then a few more and I was now just a bit merry, and in about half an hour would be facing an audience of about 8000 screaming young people, at the same time going out live on air. Well, the moment of truth came pretty quickly, and suddenly I was announced on stage. I sang the Bobby Vee hit single, "The Night has a Thousand Eyes", and to my relief it all went very well, except half way through I did forget some words, but nobody had noticed, and I got away with it. This was one show I will never ever forget; it was a tremendous thrill to sing at The Royal Albert Hall.

One other interesting show I should mention is the thirteen-week series I did with The Nu-Notes called 'Ring a Ding Ding'. It was compered by a very nice Canadian man called Pat Campbell, and he came up with an idea to create some additional interest and to give me more credibility. Each week he would interview me between songs about an imaginary conversation with Elvis Presley during the past week. We did of course work out a new script for this each week, and it was a great success. People really did believe that I was phoning Elvis every week for a chat, just amazing!

I think this would be the right time in my story for me to

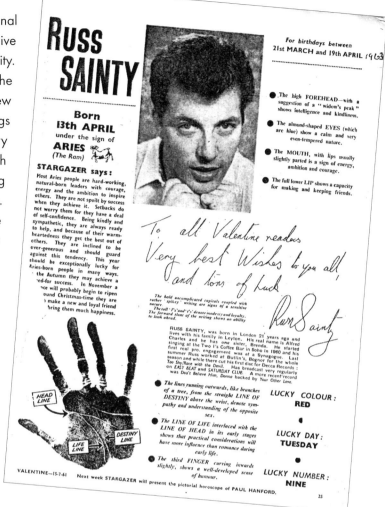

pay tribute and give my thanks to all those BBC producers who had the confidence in myself and the group, to enable me to say that Russ Sainty and The Nu-Notes are proud to have been probably the most broadcast pop group of the '60s era, and I name those I can recall – Jimmy Grant, Brian Matthew, Cyril Drake, Brian Willy, Ron Belchiar, Francis Line, Bernie Andrews, Derek and Doreen Davis, who worked together as a team and I believe were a married couple. My last BBC broadcast was sometime during 1966, a year after Russ Sainty and The Nu-Notes had disbanded. However, I have to say that over the years and even to this day the Beeb still play my records. These days it's thanks to dear Brian Matthew and his Saturday morning show "Sounds of the Sixties" – long may he and the programme continue!

The year 1961 was indeed another bumper year for me at the 'Cali', which itself was now the place to appear. Yes indeed, the California Ballroom had

Russ and The Group on the big stage at the 'Cali', 1961.

well and truly arrived and every performer wanted to be seen at this great venue, even the Yanks. By now I felt a part of the Green family, who were always very kind to me. Let's also not forget that Edwina Green, who would be about 16 years old, was doing a great job as a vocalist singing with The Ray Miller Orchestra, not bad for a young lady who helped her father build up the place. I also have fond memories of Little Dennis, who for a long time I thought was the General Manager.

It was during this year that a young lady, who always stood at the front whilst I was singing, asked me if she could run my fan club. Her name was Rosemary Smith. As things turned out, my sister Brenda and another good friend did most of the work, with contributions from Rosemary. It really was very humbling when I think back to the fantastic fan base that I had in the area, which grew like Topsie week after week. It is now of course my hope and dreams that many of those wonderful fans and friends from those heady days will see my story in the shops and take a copy home for a good nostalgic read! On 12th August 1960 The Barron Knights made their first appearance at the 'Cali' and immediately became good friends with myself and The Rhet Stoller Group, as they were now known. Barron and the boys, including Judge, who played Vibes in those early days, became our greatest fans, and were never too proud to ask questions about the sounds we were able to get, etc. Well, I have to say, it wasn't long before The Knights were making records, and the rest, as they say, is history. Well done, Duke and the Knights, I have also been a long time fan of yours, as you well know. Keep Rockin!

Now if 1960 had been a biggy for me at the 'Cali', take a deep breath, because I'm about to reveal that in the year 1961 I was booked at the 'Cali' no less than (66) sixty six times, which equates to 132x45-minute sets. Wow! And The Beatles and Stones are still in nappies! Sorry guys, only kidding!

Before we step out of the year 1961, which for us as a group has been the busiest yet and I have to say extremely exciting, I want to recall just what it was like for us when actually performing on stage at the 'Cali' during those early days. You have only to look at the photographs of us performing on the opening night of 12th March 1960 to get a feel of the atmosphere which we created, every member of the group giving every ounce of energy and drive to what was happening on that night, and it continued to be simply magic. Whilst myself, Mel Miller, Bernie Martin and Roy Toft were cavorting around the stage for all the up tempo rock numbers, unlike any other group, our lead guitarist Rhet

Rhet Stoller and Russ decide to take it easy when performing a ballad at the 'Cali', 1961.

1961—1962

Compliments of the Season
from

california Pool
WHIPSNADE ROAD
Ballroom · Dunstable

Best wishes for a Merry Christmas
and a Happy and Prosperous
New Year

Thanking our Patrons for their support in the past years and
assuring you of our best endeavours to dispense
Happiness & Entertainment in the New Year

Stoller was for the most part sitting down! Yes indeed. Completely unorthodox, but it worked. I can recall Rhet sitting down playing the number "Caravan" and we would have a massive crowd around the stage, just mesmerised at our performance – their reaction was just incredible. We would come off stage after our second 45-minute spot, completely exhausted, with adrenaline flowing like the river Thames, but it was such great fun with a feeling of satisfaction and achievement. There is nothing better for any performer than to know that your audience has enjoyed your efforts.

...enting you
...of our Christmas and
New Year's Programme of Attractions

December 15th, Friday. 8 p.m. till 11.30 p.m.
GRAND ROCK-A-CHA-CHA DANCE.
JACKIE LYNTON with Bob Xavier and The Jury.
DEAN BRENT and the Original Strollers.
Saturday, 16th. 8 p.m. till midnight.
GRAND SATURDAY NIGHT DATE.
GEOFF STOKES' ORCHESTRA.
Sunday, 17th. 7.30 p.m. until 10 p.m.
Adon White BINGO CLUB.
Wednesday, 20th. BINGO CLUB, 7.30 till 10 p.m.
Thursday, 21st. 7 p.m. for 7.35 p.m. till 10 p.m.
Great-International WRESTLING CONTEST.
including BILLY TWO RIVERS.   5/- to 12/6.
Friday, 22nd. 8 p.m. till Midnight.
English Electric Apprentices Association.
OPEN INVITATION DANCE.   TWO BANDS.   6/6.
Saturday, 23rd. 8 p.m. till Midnight.
Your Saturday DATE.
GEOFF STOKES' ORCHESTRA.
RUSS SAINTY & RHET STOLLER GROUP.
SUNDAY, 24th. 7.30 p.m. till 10 p.m.
Christmas Hamper, Grand BINGO NIGHT.
CHRISTMAS DAY. PETROL PUMPS OPEN. 10 a.m. till 2 p.m.
TUESDAY, 26th. 8 p.m. till Midnight.
2nd GRAND BOXING NIGHT PARTY   5/6.
and a Christmas present for everyone.
Great FLOOR SHOW comprising:—
SIX LOVELY FARROW GIRLS
in a non-stop three-part dancing act.
JOHNNY MAXIM. The GREAT VIRTUOSO
of the Harmonica.
THE REGENCY TWINS (in person)
Identical Twin Girl Act as appearing on same night in
'PANTOMANIA' on Television.
NORMAN TOMKINS, Xylophonist Exceptional,
with his pianist.
ARTHUR HILL from Windmill Theatre.
TOMMY THOMPSON'S ORCHESTRA.
RUSS SAINTY and RHET STOLLER GROUP.
Dancing till Midnight.

Wednesday, 27th. 7.30 till 10 p.m.
ADON WHITE. BINGO CLUB, and
GIFTS, and Fun with the Staff.

Friday, 29th. 8 p.m. till 11.30 p.m.
SUPER NON-STOP ROCK DANCE
ROBB STORME. Television and Recording Star with the
WHISPERS, also that Super Recording Group,
THE SPIRITS.

Saturday, 30th. 8 p.m. till Midnight.
Your Saturday Night Date.
RAY MILLER'S ORCHESTRA.
RUSS SAINTY and the RHET STOLLER GROUP.
Your Saturday Club Recording favourites.

Sunday, December 31st. 7.30 p.m. till 10.30 p.m.
SPECIAL BINGO CLUB 2/6
NEW YEAR GIFTS

11 p.m. till 2 a.m.   NEW YEAR SUPER NIGHT CLUB
JOHN CHAPMAN, Britain's most versatile Organist,
on the California Organ, with
ARTHUR HILL at the Grand Piano.
Midnight—' Auld Lang Syne.'
GEOFF STOKES' ORCHESTRA.
THE VERNON SISTERS. Dancing Wonders.
Norman Tomkins, Crazy Xylophonist with
Arthur Hill at the Piano.
Those Dancing Lovelies,
The SIX FARROW GIRLS on Non-Stop Revue in three
acts, with JULIE HOBBS the social Soubrette.
DANCING till 2 a.m. Extension till 1.30 a.m.
Admission to Recital and Night Club, 8/6.

...ill 10 p.m.
...LUB.

Thursday, January 4th. 7 p.m. for 7.45 till 10 p.m.
International Wrestling.
Friday, January 5th, 8 p.m.
SCREAMING LORD SUCH AND THE SAVAGES.
THE JESTERS.
Saturday, January 6th, 8 p.m.
EMILE FORD AND THE CHECKMATES.
RAY MILLER ORCHESTRA.

BUILT on side of Dunstable Downs, used and named by the
Ancient Britons CALIFORNIA, we provide all-the-year-round
Recreation and Social Events for all ages every week as follows:—
Swimming. March till September.
Roller Skating. March till September.
Roller Hockey matches each Sunday afternoon.
Tuesday nights. Amateur Wrestling. 1/6. 7 p.m.
Wednesdays, Bingo. 2/6. 7.30 p.m.
Thursdays alternate weeks. Professional Wrestling.
Fridays, Rock-a-Cha-Cha. 8 p.m. 3/6.
Saturdays. Dancing non-stop. 6/6.
Sundays. Bingo. 2/6.

Various Rooms for hire from 15 to 1,000 for Dances, Banquets,
Weddings.

Proprietors:
E. W. Green (Dunstable) Ltd.
Secretary: Miss P. Pugh.   Manager: Mr. Denis Allen.
Telephones: Box Office 62804.   Foyer 62010.
Filling Station, National Benzole, opens 7 a.m.

Printed by W. F. Bunker & Co., 2nd, Chapel Street, Luton.

Of course, as time went by our performances changed, and by 1962, with experience under our belts, we became a far more seasoned and rounded act, able to cope with all circumstances. However, the factors that didn't change were our enthusiasm and dedication to give a great show every time we went on stage. It was surely these qualities that our boss at the 'Cali', Mr Green, had seen in us right from that very first meeting at a gig in Romford on a cold winter's night, early 1960.

above Russ Sainty and The Rhet Stoller Group in action on the 'Cali''s big stage, 1961.
below The end of a good night at the 'Cali', left to right, Mr Julian Stoller, Bernie Martin, Rhet Stoller, Roy Toft, Russ Sainty, Mad Mel Miller and, in the background, Dave Taberer, a fan (friend) who fixed all our electrical breakdowns.

Chapter Eight

TRYING TO MAKE IT BIG

L ife in general is changing; the pace of life is getting faster, more traffic on the roads. Young people are more positive, sex and free love is becoming acceptable, innocence and naivety are on the way out, drugs are on the increase.

At around this time, Rhet Stoller and our drummer Bernie Martin decide to split from myself, Mel Miller and Roy Toff. This is something that was always going to happen after Barry Stoller had become Rhet, and let's face it, his record of "Chariot" had reached no. 26 in the hit parade and none of my records to date had done as well, so there was always that little bit of undercurrent from Rhet thinking he could be a star as a guitarist. He and Bernie then start to get work with Terry Dean and Jess Conrad and form a group called The Dynamics. Meanwhile Russ Sainty needs to get two performers to replace Rhet and Bernie, which was not going to be easy as they were both very good. Firstly, we get a drummer from Leyton to stand in as a temporary measure, and on guitar we manage to get Les Bennett, who played for the great Lonnie Donegan. This was OK, but we knew we had to get more permanent group members as soon as possible. After a couple of weeks, we auditioned a very young drummer from Aylesbury – Nigel Menday was his name, a very self assured young fellow, slightly cocky, but he was very good for his age. I told him he was in the group but would need to work hard to improve, and to his credit he did just that. At the same time, I got to know that a good friend from the 2 i's Coffee Bar days was looking

above Russ Sainty, at home 27 Simonds Road, Leyton, London E10, doing some work in his back bedroom office.
left A studio portrait of the new Nu-Notes line-up; back left is of course Mel Miller, who now plays electric bass guitar and vocals, Russ Sainty centre, with Roger Dean back right, our new lead guitarist. Bottom left is our new drummer from Aylesbury, Nigel Menday, and on the right is Roy Toft, rhythm guitar and vocals. 1962.

to join a group or band. His name was Big Jim Sullivan (guitarist). Jim had been with Marty Wilde and The Wild Cats for a long time and then formed a new group called The Crew Cats, and they were extremely good, in fact they had a hit instrumental with a number called "Trambone". This was a real winner for me, because Big Jim had already got himself a 'Big' reputation for his brilliant guitar playing, and could only help to boost our bookings. Jim agreed to join The Nu-Notes. Of course just running the group and doing all the bookings and paper work, together with all the driving, and running what was now a big fan club, was all getting a bit too much for me, so I asked an old friend if he would be interested to help out in this direction, which he was very happy to do. His name, Derek Jolly, stage name Derek Day. He was a sort of manager for the Buddy Monroe Five, you'll remember them from 1957, the skiffle group I first sang with. Derek was himself a singer, but for some reason was not working. He would come to my house each morning, go straight upstairs to my little office and get on with whatever needed doing, including the running of our fan club and the running of RMB Music Ltd., a company which we had formed some months previously. In fact Russ Sainty and The Nu-Notes were, I believe, the first pop group to run themselves as a company.

For a long time now, all of our bookings have come in from our reputation, but I felt it was time to place ourselves with a top London agent. I went to see Mr Tito Burn, who at this time was agent for Cliff Richard, and he was happy to put us on his books. And I have to say, bookings did improve and we found ourselves now doing Sunday concerts at some of the big seaside resorts, like Yarmouth and Torquay, but whilst this was all going along sweetly, I did not now have a record contract and that really worried me. I knew that by now I should have had a hit record – it would mean everything to me and my career.

Out of the blue, I get the opportunity to make a record, but it's only a Woolworth's record. In those days, Woolworth's would put out copy records of recent hits, on their own Embassy Label. I agreed to do it for a fee, but not in my own name! It was decided I would cover a hit by Billy Fury called "Last Night Was Made for Love", and an Adam Faith hit called "As You Like It", and my name would be Johnny Chester. The recording session went OK, and I believe the single sold well.

As summer approaches, Big Jim Sullivan tells me he will be leaving the group to take up full time session work within a couple of days. He said he was happy working with me and The Nu-Notes, but session work would make him a lot more money. Well, that's fair enough. I thanked Jim for all he had done and we are still good friends to this day; in fact I went to see him playing a jazz set a while ago at Havant in Hampshire and he was tremendous!

I need to get a new lead guitarist quick! I am told about a young guy who works in a furniture store at Tottenham Court Road, London, so make enquiries. Sure enough, the info. was correct and I asked him if he would audition for me and the rest is history. His name, Roger Seed, but his stage name would be Roger Dean. He was a very good guitarist and fitted in straightaway, and his immediate contribution was his willingness to find good guitar arrange-

A very rare occasion, Russ playing guitar on the big stage at the 'Cali' Year 1962.

ments for himself and so make us all sound that much better. With The Nu-Notes now settled, I decide to have a go at song writing. I thought this may well be the way forward, to try and compose my own hit songs, make demos of them and take them to all the main record companies in the hope of getting a new contract. I managed to write several numbers and I got the boys to put an arrangement around them, after which we would go to a small cheap studio and make a demo of each song. The first song I wrote was inspired by Ann, as you would expect with a title like "I've Got a Girl", and the next one was I guess through the same inspiration and called "What do you Know About That?".

overleaf, left A fun photo of Russ with the new line-up; it is once again Russ Sainty and The Nu-Notes, 1962.
overleaf, right Russ with the Boys at a charity bowls match in North London, 1962.

'Pop' singer opens Scouts' hall

It was a proud moment for Scouts and Cubs. Scouters and parents of the 1st Theydon Garnon troop on Saturday when their hut at Stewards Green Road, Epping was officially opened.

The hut was taken from the old gasworks at Bower Hill, rebuilt and renovated and the opening by 'pop' singer Russ Sainty, saw the realisation of their objective.

The money raised by a fete and barbecue held in conjunction with the opening of the hut will go towards the fund set up to raise the £500 needed for the site. Practically all the goods on the stalls were given by parents who also helped man various sideshows.

Opening the hut, Russ Sainty said the occasion was made extra happy for him because it also marked the date of the release of his first record for a year — "Keep Your Love Locked Up."

Summer 1962, Russ opens a new Boy Scouts hut at Epping in Essex; a great day was had by all who attended.

I decided to try the big boys, namely EMI, located at Manchester Square London. I had made an appointment to see Mr Walter Ridley, who was the Artistes Recording Manager, "A&R" for short, for HMV Records. I played him the demos of my songs, and I was really chuffed when he said he thought they were very good. However, he did not think either of them strong enough to be an A side of a new record and he didn't offer me a contract, but he promised to contact me should he find a good song and assured me that my songs would be recorded. Well, I went home with mixed feelings but I felt hopeful that this may well work out alright.

1962

" Pop " singer Russ Sainty (standing, second from left) and his backing group, who appeared at Dunstable on Saturday, called at Bletchley to see their greatest fans, Mr. and Mrs. D. Smith, of 50 Buckingham-road. The Smith children, too, are Sainty fans. Next month the Smiths go on an unusual holiday—touring Scotland with the singer and his group—the Nu Notes—and travelling in the band coach, with Mr. Smith, a driving instructor, taking a turn at the wheel.—DJ4575.

Our agent then tells me, "Russ, I've booked you a nice two-week tour of Scotland for July." Oh no! not Scotland after the last time. I really don't fancy this at all, but it's work, so I guess we need to take it. By now Ann, the girl I'm in love with, has moved back to London to be near me and finds a flat very close to where all my group live; it's in Bethune Road, Stamford Hill, London. She was a little disappointed when I told her we would soon be going to Scotland, but knew it was only for two weeks. However on the positive side, two of our greatest

fans, Greta and Dennis Smith, who live locally in Bletchley and are regulars at the 'Cali' whenever we are appearing, have decided they would love to come to Scotland with us and help share the driving. Dennis was a driving instructor after all! This was good news, because they were a lovely couple and we were delighted to think that fans, now good friends, would take things to the extreme and travel with us for the whole of our Scottish tour, Rock on!

Photo taken in 1962 showing Mel and Roy cleaning our minibus outside my house, I did help, honest!

Russ and The Nu-Notes catching a bus to their gig. Well, a group has gotta do what a group's gotta do. The show must go on, 1962.

After a week or so, I get a call from Walter Ridley's assistant, who tells me that he has got a good song, and it may well be suitable for our first single. He asked me to get the boys together and make my way up to Soho's Great Windmill Street, London, where he would meet us in a small upstairs rehearsal room. I called all the boys, and we made our way up to Soho; we found the correct address and unloaded our equipment. This was not the best of areas for parking a mini bus, even in 1962, but we did find a spot eventually. We listen to the song on tape, which was called "Keep Your Love Locked", and after about an hour it was sounding pretty good, but I had mixed feelings as to whether or not it was good enough to be a hit. Furthermore, I still believed my two songs were better.

Well, as we make preparations for our Scottish tour, and with only a few days to go before we set off, I get a call from Walter Ridley at HMV Records, and he wants us to get into the studio as soon as possible to record what will be our first single with EMI Ltd. A three-hour afternoon session is booked, and off we go to the famous Abbey Road Studios, made more famous a little later by a new group with a strange name, The Beatles. Well, we record two songs, one of which is my own composition, "I've Got A Girl", and to be very honest I believe it is my own song that should be an A side, but at this stage Mr Ridley was not making any decision – he said he would wait until the two tracks had been fully produced.

OK, with a record to be released very soon, we start our journey north to Scotland and make a stop at Perth for a few hours sleep. The following morning, we set off via the coast road to Aberdeen, and then across to Elgin, and so on to Lossiemouth and our bed and breakfast accommodation. Our gig list looks horrendous, with very long journeys to many of the towns we are to play, one of which involves us travelling from Lossie all the way down the west coast to the peninsular town of Campbell Town. On the positive side we have the opportunity to see some fantastic scenery and wildlife, driving all over the Highlands of Scotland, just magic!

It's on one of these long trips, whilst listening to the BBC Radio Don Coster show, that we hear him mention Russ Sainty, and next we hear our new record being played. Woowie! This is fantastic – we stop the bus and turn the radio up very loud, all of us listening intently, with big smiles all round, then, as it ended, we all cheered. However, for the next hour or so, we had an inquest on what we had heard. We all agree it was OK, but nothing like what we last heard in the studio. They had taken off The Nu-Notes' vocal backings and put on The Mike Sams Singers' female voices. And these are on a very big echo sound, which had completely changed what we had originally done in the studio. Of course, at this stage we have no idea how my own song on the B side might sound. None of us feel too sure about this, but we are happy to know that we do once again have a single on the market.

Teenage Topics
By HELEN and DICK

A few weeks after writing about Mrs. Mills, that cheerful chubby pianist, having been born in Bletchley we have discovered that another show business celebrity has a local connection.

Russ Sainty, a popular performer at Wilton Hall, Bletchley, and the California Ballroom, Dunstable, spent the war years in the village of Woughton. Russ and his family were evacuated from their Leyton, London, home and lived at Kings Cottage, Woughton. His father, Alfred, worked in the Bletchley Post Office for part of the war years.

Russ and his backing group, the Nu Notes, appeared at Wilton Hall last Saturday. He is now 24 and has been tipped for stardom by one of Britain's top song writers, Johnny Worth, who has written ten songs for Adam Faith and Eden Kane. Russ appears on the popular radio shows, "Saturday Club," and "Easy Beat," and plays at ballrooms and theatres all over the county.

Less than three years ago Russ was in a very different profession. He was a Horticulturist, growing flowers and shrubs for Leyton's town park. But all this changed when in 1959 he was persuaded to enter a talent contest at the Rialto Cinema, Leyton. He won and then joined show business.

He still lives in Leyton with his parents and younger sister, Brenda. When he left school at 15 he was all set to be a jockey and began training at Newmarket but was fired for putting on too much weight.

Not Crazy On Rock

MR. SMITH says he is a Russ Sainty fan not because he's crazy on rock 'n' roll, but because he likes his voice and also likes him as a person.

Mother-in-law, Mrs. Nancy Smith, of Kennet-drive, Bletchley, is also a fan. Unfortunately she gets very little opportunity of seeing him, for she volunteers to look after her grandchildren—aged between eight and two—while her son and daughter-in-law go rockin'.

The children also are ardent fans. One night last week Russ was appearing on a late-night television programme and the youngest daughter kept crying. But she was quiet immediately she was told that Uncle Russ was on television.

Band Tour Holiday

RUSS and his group, the Nu-Notes, scored a great success at Wilton Hall, Bletchley, on Saturday of last week. Before the session they spent the afternoon with the Smith family.

Early next month Mr. and Mrs. Smith are going on an unusual holiday. They are touring Scotland with the singer and his group. They will travel in the band coach, Mr. Smith taking turns to drive.

A last word from Mrs. Smith: "I never went mad on a pop singer before to the extent of following him around. But Russ Sainty is marvellous and will be a top one day."

MAINLY FOR WOMEN
By HELEN

Fans Of Russ Sainty

SATURDAY night dances, with electric guitars and jiving, twisting bodies are generally associated with teenagers, but almost every week-end a Bletchley housewife and her driving instructor husband leave their home at 50 Buckingham-road to attend such dances all over the country. And they are no teenage couple. Greta Smith, aged 28, and her 30-years-old husband, Dennis, have three young children and a business to run. Mr. Smith owns the Viceroy Driving School.

There is yet another unusual aspect of this couple's week-end activities. They don't just go to any old rock session. They attend only those where singer, Russ Sainty, is appearing. Not only are they great fans of the singer, but personal friends.

Mrs. Smith says, "It all started a year ago. I was up to my elbows in washing one Saturday when Dennis came in and said that we were going to a dance. My mother-in-law came over to look after the children and off we went to the California Ballroom, Dunstable. There I heard Russ Sainty for the first time. Frankly, I had never heard of him, but I was immediately struck by his personality and talent. Since that time I have followed him regularly."

July 1962

Two records in two months for Leyton's Russ Sainty

"ALMOST two years without a record—now two in two months," said Leyton pop singer Russ Sainty on Friday.

On July 27 his "comeback" record was released by H.M.V. titled "Keep Your Love Locked." Now while this disc is still being played on radio and TV disc programmes a second record is being issued by H.M.V.

"It was all done in a big rush. Just over a week ago I got a call from my record company asking me to record a new American number," said Russ.

Reason for the urgency was the fact that the song — "Send Me The Pillow" — has already reached a high placing in the American charts. It is expected to sell well over here as well.

Song-writer Russ Sainty — he wrote "I've Got a Girl", the number which backs his earlier record — has also written and composed the flip on his new disc. The title? "What Do You Know?"

The record is being released on September 21, although advance copies of the disc have already been sent to disc jockeys and television producers.

The Sainty backing group — The Nu Notes — also hope to cut a disc shortly. They have not recorded an instrumental number since — "Chariot," reached 19th position in the charts over two years ago.

HERE AND THERE

Chigwell Folk Club — which opened its winter series recently — plans a gigantic folk and jazz concert for the near future.

Sole object of the club secretary says the club is to raise money to pay the fees of name artists for appearances at weekly club nights.

Already, in less than [...]

the club's membership [...] Each [...]

NEW H.M.V & CAPITOL SINGLES
ORDER NOW FROM YOUR LOCAL E.M.I DEPOT OR FACTOR

HMV	Weekly releases for JULY 27th 1962 (Release No. 438)

BRIAN HYLAND
Sealed with a kiss
Summer job — 45-POP1051

MINUCCI and Orchestra
Summer Nocturne
Madeira — 45-POP1052

BARRY BARNETT
My love
When you're young and
Only seventeen — 45-POP1053

JOHN LEYTON
Down the River Nile
I think I'm falling in love — 45-POP1054

RUSS SAINTY with The Nu Notes
Keep your love locked (deep in your heart) with the Michael Sammes Singers
I've got a girl — 45-POP1055

TIM CONNOR
Without a shoulder to cry on
I've fallen in love (both film 'She knows y'know') — 45-POP105[...]

Capitol CAPITOL	Weekly releases for JULY 27th 1962 (Release No. 438)

JACK SCOTT
I can't hold your letters (in my arms)
Sad story — 45-CLI5[...]

VIC DAMONE
With Billy May and his Orchestra
Vieni, vieni
Cathy (from MGM film 'Boys' Night Out') — 45-CLI5[...]

Russ Sainty back on the disc scene with a potential hit

TODAY (Friday) is a red letter day for Leyton singer Russ Sainty. It is the day when his first record on the H.M.V. label is released.

Formerly a Decca recording artist, Russ has not recorded for over a year. Now he comes back into the disc scene with "Keep Your Love Locked"—a beat ballad which is a potential hit.

Things have moved fast for Russ Sainty and his backing group. The Nu-Notes, in the past month. After successfully passing a recording test at the end of June they waited for a number to record. Within a week they were back at the recording studios, running through a new American song.

The disc was cut on July 6— the day before Russ and his group left for Scotland on a 14-day tour of one-night stands.

Although Russ has been aired regularly on top-rated radio shows (Easy Beat and Saturday Club), he has had little luck record-wise. The Nu-Notes, however, have been more successful. They waxed "Chariot," an instrumental number which made the charts last year.

Own song

The Nu-Notes back Russ on "Keep Your Love Locked" and also on the flip. "I've Got A Girl" — a song written and composed by Russ Sainty.

Without a record, Russ has been unable to get television appearances, but that's changing now. On Tuesday he was spotlighted on Scottish Television's "Downbeat."

After the show he flew back to London to prepare for a "Ring A Ding Ding" radio airing on July 31.

On August 5 he is booked to appear on "Easy Beat" and on August 25 on "Saturday Club". Other top radio and television bookings are also being negotiated for him in conjunction with the promotion of his new disc.

Charles Blackwell for the States

Charles Blackwell — who wrote and composed the Mike Sarne hit "Come Outside" — may well be flitting regularly between Britain and the States in the near future.

This Walthamstow musician — whose session bands provide the backing music to hit records — has had offers to back American artists.

"Nothing is finally settled but I am flying to the States shortly to do a couple of sessions," said Charles who has now written the follow-up disc to 'Come Outside'.

Since the disc climbed the charts there have been several offers for the future. "I may well become a freelance recording manager, or I may start my own recording company — or if I get a hit record with my own orchestra I may well tour," he told me.

Charles Blackwell made his debut as a recording manager when he conducted and produced a Decca session with the Vernon Girls this week.

Mike Sarne's follow-up disc is "Will I What?" and "Birds — I Love Yer".

D. P.

TOP TEN

1 I Remember You
Frank Ifield
2 Can't Stop Loving You
Ray Charles
3 Here Comes That Feeling
Brenda Lee
4 Speedy Gonzales
Pat Boone
5 Come Outside
Mike Sarne
6 Ya Ya Twist
Petula Clark
7 Looking Out The Window
Cliff Richard
8 Good Luck Charm
Elvis Presley
9 Right Said Fred
Bernard Cribbins
10 Yes My Darling Daughter
Edye Gorme

Year 1962, photo showing Russ performing for the BBC. The programme being Easy Beat, recorded at the Playhouse Theatre London; note the musical director on the left, Bert Weedon.

Now, with only a couple of days still to do, I am in for a big shock! Whilst we are having a bit to eat in our usual cafe/restaurant in Elgin, I see walking towards me two familiar faces – my mouth drops, I'm in shock. It's Ann and Joy, Roy's girlfriend, who was a dancer at Butlins. I grab Roy and point towards the two girls, but he too is in shock. "What the heck are you doing up here?" I said to Ann, who replied, "We thought we would hitch-hike up here to see you." I said, "But Ann, didn't you realise how much danger you were both in?" This is crazy. After all the huffing and puffing, we had a kiss and a cuddle and it was nice to have the girls with us, but in just two more days we would be making our way back home.

Our last night was a concert in Aberdeen, and it was such a pleasant change to do a performance to a sit down audience in a very nice auditorium, the name of which I cannot recall. With a successful show over, we load the bus, and the boys prepare for the long journey home. Meanwhile, Ann and I will stay overnight and catch an early flight from Aberdeen Airport to London, Heathrow. This was necessary because I had to do a BBC broadcast that same evening.

above Russ and Bert Weedon at the Beeb in relaxed mood, year 1962.
below Russ with The Brook Brothers rehearsing for a broadcast with the BBC, 1962.

above Russ trying to play none other than Kenny Ball's trumpet. All in a day's work when recording a show for the Beeb. Year 1962.

left "The Man", Brian Matthew, Mr BBC, preparing Russ for a recording of Easy Beat, 1962.

We all needed a few days off to
recover from what had been a hectic couple of weeks –
there is no rest for the wicked, as the saying goes. Our agent, Tito Burns, is
on the phone giving me a list of bookings for the next month, but at this stage
with no TV, which we needed to plug our record. Ann by now had moved to
a nice flat in Putney, and was working in London's Bond Street at the famous
Goray Skirts establishment, modelling, of course, skirts! At about this time, I
am contacted by Tommy Sanderson, a session pianist and music publisher
I know very well, who wants to speak to me about a recording, but with a
difference. He wants me to record the hit song "Go Away Little Girl" and then
do a day's filming at Elstree Studios, after which the completed recording
and film of me singing would be put into a new type of Juke Box Machine
– I believe it was called a "Cine-Box"? The idea was to watch the singer
on a small screen whilst the recording was being played, and it cost one
shilling, that's about five pence today. It was a novel idea, but didn't really
take off and, unlike the Juke Box, these were few and far between, and soon
disappeared. I am, however, very proud to have been one of the few singers
who has actually done this, and so become a tiny part of music history!

It is September 1962, HMV Records have decided our last record is not going to make it as a hit, and they want me back into EMI Abbey Road Studios urgently. Walter Ridley tells me he has a hit song, and it should suit me down to the ground. That same day, I rush up to his office to run through the song, and he booked three hours' studio time immediately. The song was called "Send Me the Pillow (That You Dream On)". A country song which was flying up the charts in the U.S.A., recorded by pop star Johnny Tillotson, who had already had a smash hit with his single, "Poetry in Motion". It would now be a race to get my single on the market before his version is released in England. That's the way it worked in those days.

When I arrived at Abbey Road Studios, I walked in to see at least a thirty-piece orchestra together with The Mike Sams Singers, and conducting the lot was Frank Barber. After recording "The Pillow", I hear my own song "What do you Know About That" run through as a rehearsal, and I thought it sounded great. We then record my song, and the session is complete. As a matter of interest, the recording engineer for this, and some of my other recordings at Abbey Road, was a fellow who later had a big hit record of his own. His name was Hurricane Smith, and I believe his big hit single was called "Oh Babe".

My new single is a rush release, and EMI really pull out all the stops to promote me. I do several Friday Night Spectaculars for Radio

12—EVENING ARGUS, WEDNESDAY, AUGUST 15, 1962

SPIN WITH ME by Anne Nightingale

Meet Russ, the company man

Who kept chickens in his office

RUSS DAINTY

THERE are several ways to become a pop singer, most of them well and truly flogged. But if you want an off-beat method, you can do what 24-year-old Russ Sainty did.

He formed a company. Made himself chairman. And announced the company's aims—the furtherance of Russ Sainty. The company carries on the business of managing and booking dates for Russ.

★　☆　★

"It's best this way," he told me. "I've got a typewriter, a telephone, headed notepaper, a filing system, biographies, pictures and fan club material.

"It's cost me a couple of hundred quid so far, even if things have got a bit tight sometimes—

for instance, I checked the bank balance the other day and found we were down to 1s. 11d.!

"I once kept 70 chicken in the office. I'd bought them in Petticoat Lane, so I couldn't very well leave them outside, could I?" he asked.

Of course not, I murmured.

"Then they grew bigger. So I had to evict them into the garden . . ."

And then?

"Why, nothing . . ."

Mr. Sainty has been on tangents all his life. At 15 he was going to be a jockey. Went down to Newmarket to train. They paid him five shillings a week. But he spent it all on food. Put on too much weight. Sacked. Then he joined a borough council as a horticulturist. He didn't quite dig the name—but enjoyed the work planting shrubs in the council gardens.

A skiffle group claimed his

(H.M.V.) Not bad. Not bad at all. But not, I fear, good enough to hit the jackpot.

．．．．．

August 1962

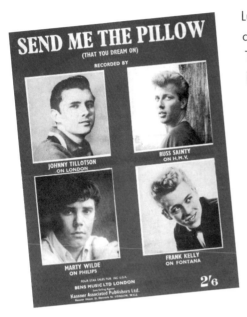

Luxemburg, Tito Burns lines up TV appearances all over the place, I am on Anglia and Border TV, Welsh and Scottish TV, Channel Islands TV, just to mention a few. Together with this, I have my almost weekly BBC radio broadcasts, so it really was all happening. It is now October '62, and EMI's HMV Records line up a very special competition as part of promoting my single. I am to record a Friday Night Spectacular, and during my interview with Muriel Young, we will be asking our Radio Luxemburg listeners to write in with some answers to questions about me, and the winner will get a fantastic trip to London as the guest of EMI. She will win *The Pillow That I Dream On!*

Promoting my new single, 1962.

Maltese Composer At R.M.B.
MEETS 'PRO' POP SINGER

➥ Maltese composer and writer Joe Bellizzi of Lija, who is in U.K. has not been lucky enough with British disc companies in an effort to induce them publish some of his works but struck water in the desert when he visited the R.M.B. Music Limited in Simmonds Road Leyton, London. He wanted to see the chairman and climbed two flights of stairs to a bedroom in a terraced house in East London. And on the door it says: "R.M.B. Music Ltd." The chairman: Russ Sainty, 24, a professional pop singer. The directors: they are drawn from his accompanying group, the Nu Notes.

R.M.B. Music Ltd. is a small, but live-wire office. Here is what the "Daily

RUSS SAINTY

"Mirror" says about Russ Sainty: "Chairman Russ is a do-it-yourself-kid. In his bed-

room is a map of Britain. Green pins mark 200 cities and towns where Russ has sung; yellow pins pick out the areas where the Russ Sainty Fan Club thrives"

His latest records are "Keep your love locked" with the 'B' side having "I've Got a Girl", which he himself wrote. Russ and the Nu Notes have made their bow on H.M.V.

By the way, Russ has been much interested in Joe Bellizzi's work and may publish one or two of his compositions. That is why Joe broke the ice. Joe speaks highly of Russ who, besides being a recording star, is a real treat in B.B.C.'s Saturday Club, Easy Beat, Twistin' Time and Ring-a-Ding-Ding.

Jimmy Grant, producer of the top-rated B.B.C. "Saturday Club" says Russ is "a really professional artist". At 24 Russ is one of Britain's most consistent beat and ballad singers. He appears with the popularity pendulum on all the top radio shows and plays to capacity audiences at ballrooms and theatres all over the country.

★   ☆   ★   ★   ☆   ★

● His accompanying group the Nu Notes — is one of London's top instrumental groups comprising bass guitarist Mel Miller (20); rhythm guitarist Roy Toft (19); drummer Nigel Menday (17); and lead guitarist Roger Brian Seed (19). (above).

The group sets the style for other groups to follow. Mel Miller is a dead ringer for the late Buddy Holly and is often mistaken for the talented Buddy (killed in an air crash). Roy Toft played with the Checkmates before joining Russ.

Spotlight On Variety
— By —
Fred Barry

A RESIDENT

Title of the A-side: "Because of Love" (Decca). And it must surely become a resident of Pop Thirty—because of love. . . .

THERE has been a similar outpouring of affection in the United States for singer Johnny Tillotson.

He is having success with a song called "Send Me The Pillow That You Dream On."

And the girls are doing just that. He is getting through the post a constant flow of pillows —with lipstick imprints —from girl fans.

Mr. Tillotson's disc comes out here tomorrow on London.

He has two British contenders singing the same song. There is Russ Sainty in form on H.M.V and a promising newcomer named Frank Kelly (Fontana).

EMI
NEW POPS

This week's 'Top' single

RUSS SAINTY

SEND ME THE PILLOW THAT YOU DREAM ON

HMV 45-POP1069

"SEND ME THE PILLOW YOU DREAM ON" urges JOHNNY TILLOTSON (London). The American singer is a regular Hit Parade visitor, and

should register again with this typical teenbeat song. Britain's RUSS SAINTY has covered it on HMV. We prefer Russ's firm voice to Tillotson's.

'MR TEN PER CENT.' SAINTY—POP TYCOON ON HIS WAY IN

ALAN GODDARD'S DISC GOSSIP

Russ Sainty manages his own affairs.

★ THE chairman of one of Britain's newest companies presides over board meetings in the back bedroom of a terraced house in East London.

The boardroom-bedroom—where 70 chicks were once raised — is equipped with a typewriter, a desk chair with a wobbly seat, a bed, and a dressing-table bulging with files of correspondence in drawers.

Long day

The room is small but throbs with activity. Most afternoons there are board meetings. Phone calls, correspondence and administration take up most of the day. Most evenings

the directors are backing the boss behind a mike at concerts and ballrooms.

Said pop singer Russ Sainty, chairman of RMB Music Ltd., "Sometimes we start at 8.30 am and don't finish until 2 am. It's a long day. But we're working for ourselves. That's the great thing.

● Russ and his directors, drawn from his group called the Nu-Notes, are probably unique in show business. They manage their own affairs, act as their own "Mr Ten Per Cent."

After two years in the singing trade, Russ found that he seemed to be getting nowhere. His records sold steadily but unspectacularly. He and his group took stock of their position early this year, decided to go it alone and sank £300 into forming their own company.

Tough

Like any other new company, the first few months have been the toughest for RMB. "It's cost us about £250 so far," said Russ. "Three weeks ago the company had exactly 1s. 11d. in the kitty."

But their livewire persistence has produced results. Without the aid of a manager, Russ broadcasts at least once a month. Every time Russ was on the air, recording chiefs

were bidden by a flood of telegrams to listen.

Finally came RMB's big break. Russ landed an HMV contract and his first disc date for more than a year. Immediately his fans (built up from 33 to 300 in six weeks) were advised by their club newsletter to buy, listen and request.

● Russ knows exactly where his fans are situated. On the wall of his nerve centre of RMB Music Ltd. is a pin-dotted map of Britain. Green pins mark the 200 towns where he has 200 towns where he has appeared. Yellow pins denote each area where there are 10 or more fan club members.

One of the targets of this likeably eager pop tycoon is the directors' box at the Leyton Orient football ground at the rear of Russ's home.

"When I'm standing in the terracing at the Orient I look up and see Cliff Richard as a regular guest of Lew and Leslie Grade in the directors' box," said Russ.

"When I'm invited into that box I'll really know that Russ and RMB have arrived."

"Keep Your Love Locked" HMV 45-POP 1055), asks Russ Sainty, but don't give the key to anyone else but me. The material is just fair. But Russ gives it all he's got. It could make the Top Twenty.

CHARLIE GRACIE *Pretty Baby; Night and Day, U.S.A.* (London HLU 9603)

REMEMBER Charlie? His big hit was "Wanderin' Eyes". Since then, not much. He has a busy backing for "Pretty Baby", heavy ponderous beat, lots of voices crashing away at the rear. Charlie seems almost dominated by the backing at times—and he also has an apparent touch of the hiccoughs, but the juke-boxes may echo to it for a few months. Too much happens for drawing-room listening.

"Night and Day" has a guitar intro, then a throaty Mr. Gracie enters, fairly pommelling the lyrics. Trouble is this sounded about five years out of date—in fact more like his work at the time of his big hit. Old-timers may go for it.

THREE ●●●

RUSS SAINTY *Send Me The Pillow You Dream On; What Do You Know About That* (HMV Pop 1069)

RUSS has a steadily-growing following through his one-nighters. He has the Johnny Tillotson opposition on "Send Me The Pillow". There's little to choose between all the versions of this harmless C and W number—in fact we don't think the song will enjoy the same success here as in the States. Russ sings simply with a lot of feeling—and we definitely like the plant version which filled in the odd gaps. Now stand by for the pillow-fight.

Flip was written by Russ—and it's a lively piece with a staccato atmosphere. Big-beat ballad material all very enjoyable but, quite honestly, not much different from umpteen similar numbers. Russ does sing well, though.

She will also win a wonderful night out with myself, Shaw Taylor and Muriel Young, where first we will have a very exciting helicopter trip over London, followed by dinner at London's famous Pigalle Restaurant, after which she will win something very special. She will be presented with The Pillow That I Dream On, yes indeed, the very same one. Come on now, no sniggering! This was a fantastic prize for any young girl in those days; you're still laughing, I just know you are! Well, the actual winner of this competition was Andrea Wood, from Gloucester, a very nice teenage girl, and I can assure you, my reader, that the whole evening went like a dream and Andrea had a really super and memorable time. As a matter of interest, I would love to know where Andrea is now, in the year 2008. Another very important and memorable thing that happened to both Andrea and me whilst flying over London that night around about 20th October 1962, with Shaw Taylor carrying a portable recording machine, was when he recorded us both talking and requesting a new song by a new group. The song was called "Love Me Do", and the group called "The Beatles". This recording was then broadcast the following week on Radio Luxemburg. I have to say, both Andrea and myself thought what a funny name, little did we know whilst doing that recording just what was to follow. I often wondered if any of the Beatles ever heard our recording. No, I've not had a thank you from that day to this. The helicopter having now

opposite Russ with competition winner Andrea Wood, about to fly over London in the helicopter, autumn 1962.

turned round over Tower Bridge, we then fly back following the River Thames towards Battersea and the helipad not far from the massive old power station; the pilot gently brings us down and our trip is over. However, waiting to pick us up was a chauffeur driven limousine. We all piled in and were then taken to the famous Pigalle Restaurant and Cabaret Club in London's Piccadilly. On arrival, we were escorted inside and taken to our table, where we joined several other EMI hierarchy, but more importantly for me, my dear old mum was also at the table, a really great surprise for me. Well, the evening was something to remember, we had the works, including of course the presentation of my autographed pillow to our competition winner, Andrea Wood. This was followed by great merriment and lots of clinking of glasses; the wine was definitely flowing, not for Andrea of course, she was far too young, but I could see my mum was getting a little worse for wear, so much so that Shaw Taylor decided to get our driver to take Mum home in the limo, all the way to Leyton. As you can imagine, my Mum never lived it down. As for the rest of us, including Andrea, we stayed the night in a London Hotel, and the next morning we all went our separate ways and a fabulous night was over, with mission achieved.

With Billy Cotton on 'Friday Spectacular'

Wins Russ Sainty's pillow

AN evening with the stars and a flight over London by night in a helicopter were among the thrills of a wonderful day for Ribston Hall High School girl Andrea Wood, of 58, The Oval.

It all began when Andrea entered a competition organised by the E M I Recording Company to mark the release of Russ Sainty's "Send me the pillow that you dream on."

Competitors were asked to say how they would like to spend an evening in London—Andrea sent in a winning answer.

Her day began when she arrived at the E M I Studios for a recording of "Friday Spectacular," in which she appears on Friday of this week with the stars.

She met Russ Sainty and received his pillow—one of Andrea's prizes. At the top he signs her autograph.

Other stars in the show were Billy Cotton, with whom she is seen above. Also in this picture are Bert Weedon and Kathy Kay.

As part of her prize Andrea said she would like to meet Russ Sainty's mother. This wish was granted. In the picture on the left Russ and his mother are seen with Andrea and Shaw Taylor, host of "Friday Spectacular."

On the right Andrea is ready to take off from Battersea heliport with Russ Sainty and Shaw Taylor. She was interviewed in the air

The day ended with an evening at the Pigalle restaurant with Russ Sainty.

Gloucester Journal Saturday 27 October 1962

above Russ Sainty, Andrea Wood, Shaw Taylor and the pilot about to board the helicopter, autumn 1962.
below Following the helicopter trip, we are seen at London's Pigalle club and restaurant at Piccadilly London. Photo showing Shaw Taylor, Andrea Wood and myself checking out the menu.

*Valentine Monday
27 October 1962*

It is not long before I hear that "Send Me the Pillow" had been recorded by two other English singers, Marty Wilde and Frank Kelly. This was a blow! I was very disappointed and, to make matters even worse, Johnny Tillotson's version was now released in England, together with yet another recording. It was the original one, recorded many years previous by Hank Locklin, who was the composer of the song. We now have five different versions of the song and that was several too many for any version to be a hit. EMI, under HMV Records, continued to plug and advertise my version, but to be honest, it was always going to be an uphill battle! Then a bit of good news. Tito Burns, my agent, calls to tell me that Russ Sainty and The Nu-Notes will do a three-week tour in October, with Bobby Vee and the Crickets. Great news! This will help promote "The Pillow". I'm still in with a chance to get my first elusive hit record. Tito tells me who else is on the tour, and The Nu-Notes will accompany all acts except one. On the bill are Bobby Vee, The Crickets, Ronnie Carroll, Johnny de Little, Frank Berry (compere) and Frank Kelly and the Hunters. I was in shock. I asked Tito Burns, "Why have you put Frank Kelly on the show? He's recorded the same song as I have done." He replied, "Well, I've had an idea, I'm going to advertise the show as the battle of the pillow boys, this should get you some great publicity." I thought OK, it's not a bad idea. Even better, because most people seem to think that my version is better than his. I could win this battle, ha ha, but I really need some kind of gimmick.

You will remember the chap running my small office and doing the fan club, Derek Day? Well, he suggested he could make a very big cut out shape of a pillar box, painted bright red, with eyes and a nose while the mouth would be the hole where you post your letters. However, in this case, I would reach into the mouth and pull out some miniature pillows, made by my sister and autographed by myself, then just throw them into the audience. OK, it's not something pop singers would do today, but in 1962 it did work, and the kids who were lucky enough to get a mini pillow were the envy of all the girls sitting around them. For sure, it kept my sister busy on her sewing machine. She must have made around 100 mini pillows for this tour alone. The tour was a real buzz. Everywhere we went, we had screaming young teenage girls following us around and crowding the stage door. It never got out of hand or over the top, just excited young girls having fun and wanting to say hello and get an autograph. Bobby Vee was a lovely guy, well mannered, well dressed and always with a good word for everyone, and to be honest everyone on the tour got on well with one another. We travelled all together in a luxury coach, after being picked up each day near Baker Street Station, London, and would be dropped off in the early hours each morning. On some of the longer trips we would stay overnight. On the long trips, everyone would have their own idea of relaxation. The Nu-Notes and I would very often rehearse new songs or songs we had composed. Ronnie Carroll, Bobby Vee and sometimes The Crickets would play cards. However, it seemed that no sooner had we begun the tour than it was rapidly coming to an end. Time flies when you're having fun!

Bobby Vee and The Crickets Tour Souvenir Programme October 1962

It's now December and the tour is over. I call Tito Burns about bookings,"What's happening?" I said to him. "We don't have much in the book until the New Year." He came out with some cock'n'bull story, as all agents do when it suits them, but apart from a few BBC Broadcasts and our regular California Ballroom bookings over the Christmas holidays, things were a bit thin.

I called a meeting with the Boys and told them we didn't have much work, and has anyone got any ideas? Roger Dean didn't seem too bothered, but Mel Miller came up with an idea for himself, together with Roy and me. Mel said, "Why don't we go to that local nursery in Leyton and buy a van load of pot plants, already wrapped, and go knocking on doors selling them for Christmas. And to make things look completely genuine and upfront, we will each wear a college type scarf and tell our potential buyer that we are students trying to make a bit of cash for Christmas." Oh yes, let's give it a go. The next day Mel, Roy and I drive to this local commercial nursery and pick up the plants at wholesale price and off we go. We choose upmarket areas and start knocking on doors! Well, I can honestly tell you, we sold a van load every day for three weeks, and at the end of it we split all the profits, which were quite considerable. OK, it was long days and bloody hard work, but I was proud of what we had done under the circumstances, and I can't think of too many groups or singers these days that would do such a thing.

Christmas plants kept Russ from workhouse!

CHRISTMAS DAY in the workhouse wasn't quite a certainty for Russ Sainty and his group. But they had to face it—prospects for the festive season were pretty bleak. The kitty was just about empty, there was no work in the offing and instalments on £1,000 worth of instruments were due for payment.

This was a couple of years ago when Russ, the 24-year-old singer from London's East End, wasn't finding dates as easy to come by as he does today, with some 200 broadcasts, one-night stands and concert tours to his credit.

So Russ, a shrewd, independent Cockney, who now runs his own management business to promote his career, drew on his experience of market gardening to provide himself and the group with some much needed ready cash.

Before he took to singing for a living, Russ was a green-fingered wizard of Leyton's Parks Department, the man responsible for the borough's display of flowers and shrubs. It is not generally known, but he has passed the Royal Horticultural Society's exam and is liable to astonish listeners by referring to plants by their Latin names.

From the tips he picked up as a gardener, Russ was well aware that there was a tidy profit to be made from the sale of plants, even though he was completely clueless about how to sell them. But a couple of quick lessons from Mel Miller, a one-time salesman turned bass guitarist, and they were ready to go.

Russ, Mel and rhythm guitarist Roy Toft piled into the Sainty van and arrived at a local nursery with the grand total of £3 19s., their combined resources, to invest in seven dozen plants, of the potted and trailing varieties, and ferns.

With college scarves slung around their necks to add respectability and authenticity, they posed as college students earning an honest penny to pay for their studies and set about bringing colour and cheer into the households of Chingford and Woodford.

From the start the plants sold like hot solanum capsicastrum (a red-berried plant popular around Christmas). The boys had bought at 1s. 6d.

each and sold their wares for a profit of one shilling. Their income each day was ploughed back into further purchases, with never more than the bare minimum taken for meals and petrol.

"We had a lot of fun," recalls Russ. "Being salesmen landed us in some embarrassing situations and it took some smart talking to edge our way out of them. For instance, if we were asked which college we were at, we said the Royal College of Music. That was all right, so long as we were not asked in for a cuppa. If we were and there was a piano or guitar available, you could bet your life that we would be asked to entertain.

"We used to tell them all sorts of stories—after all, they would have been rather surprised to have students

of the RCM play rock 'n' roll—and plead that our fingers were too cold, or that we were too short of time to stay and play."

Four days before Christmas, Russ, Roy and Mell called a halt. They counted up their takings and found that the £3 19s. they had originally invested had matured to produce a dividend of £90. The equipment was no longer in danger of being reclaimed. Instalments were paid and there was still enough left over for the partners to treat themselves.

After that their luck changed. Russ and The Nu-Notes haven't looked back. There is no danger of them being on the steps of the poorhouse this Christmas. They've plenty of work to keep them going until June.

January 1963

Now before we go into 1963, I think this would be a good spot for me to tell you a little about The Nu-Notes and myself and a sort of day-to-day snippet of what life for us was like in those heady early sixties. Sex, drugs and Rock 'n' Roll are the words, and the image that I guess most people would have in mind relating to rock and pop groups from that particular era, and I would say that this is because in the main it's an image that has been earned by those participating. However, I

Scene No.4 October 5 1962

POPS POPS POPS POPS POPS POPS POPS POPS P

They thought I was a secretary

A quiet, twenty-four-year-old from the East End of London has won a one-man battle against the closed shop world of pop music.

A year ago Russ Sainty was dropped by one of the big pop stables and told he was no longer wanted. Once he was out no-one would handle him. So Sainty, singer of *Happy Go Lucky Me* and this week's release *Send Me The Pillow You Dream On*, retired to his bedroom in Leyton and started his own music company.

The object: To promote Russ Sainty, singer. And prove Tin Pan Alley wrong.

It's been a hard fight, but with the release this week of his first record for two years he has succeeded. The telephone rang and it was Tito Burns on the line asking if he could handle all Sainty's bookings in future.

Says Sainty: 'I've been so busy lately I was only too glad. I've had to hire two secretaries, put in a new phone and buy four new chairs and a table, business has been so good.

When I was dropped no-one would touch me. They all said that

if one stable dropped me then they weren't going to take me up. There must be something wrong with me. It made me hopping mad. 'The hit parade should never be. It's a completely false judge of talent. If you have the right sound it goes and that's all there is to it. They get any old person in to produce this noise. Then they drop him when his use has been served. The hit parade is one thing, talent is another.'

When he first converted his bedroom into an office he had one

chair, a table, a phone and nobody working for him. Now he has a cream coloured phone to himself, a fan club and a flood of requests for him to appear all over Britain.

Next month he has been picked to accompany Bobby Vee on a nationwide tour.

He recalls the early days of his battle: 'I used to answer the phone and take my own bookings. The promoters who rang up did not know it was me. They thought it was a secretary. Of course I couldn't get any of the big dates. I had to be content with one night stands at dance halls. But gradually the word got round about our act.'

Outside in the street is the mini-bus he drives to one night stands. On top is an enormous white hardboard pillow advertising his record.

Another fault with the pop system, he found, was the method of record making. 'They used to rush them through,' he says. 'They didn't care what sort of a record you made as long as they got it out. Again they were just hoping for the lucky break. That's no way to go about making records. No wonder you get so much rubbish.'

With the sudden rush of intelligence into the record making industry Tin Pan Alley must sooner or later get a bit worried. It is not a commodity that has been very plentiful these last few years. But with people like Sainty and Sarne around finding out for themselves what it's all about the rubbish may be cut to a minimum in future.**Michael Wale**

am about to dispel a little bit of this image by telling you that Russ Sainty and The Nu-Notes were one of the very few Rock 'n' Roll groups who didn't really fit this accepted, standard image. Now don't be disappointed. I'm sure you were hoping for some torrid scandal stories, but the truth is, it just didn't happen to us. OK, we had our moments and a whole lot of fun, but I can honestly say nothing really bad with regard to sex and drugs. Yes, all the guys chatted up good looking females who might be hanging about after the show, but that's just normal and to be expected, and it would be fair to say that things probably went further than chatting at times, but for the most part that was about as naughty as it got. For me personally, I didn't get involved. After all, I had a girlfriend and our relationship was serious. I have to say, we were aware that many of the rock groups were taking drugs and smoking pot (grass), but it never ever came into our lifestyle. The nearest we ever got to taking drugs was on the odd occasion when Bernie Martin (drums) would take a couple of Pro Plus tablets and wash them down with a couple of glasses of barley wine. However, this was not a regular happening by any means. The truth is none of us were drinkers. The most any of us would have to drink, apart from soft drinks, would be half a pint of lager with lime. I'm sorry if this sounds pathetically boring, but it's the truth. None of us felt the need for drugs and booze, but I can assure you we had a great time and tons of laughs, but

he's Mr. Enterprise

MY Girl Friday, who is nineteen and impressionable, describes singer **Russ Sainty** as "dreamy."

My own assessment of this up-and-coming popster from Leyton, London, is that behind his pleasantly relaxed exterior lurks a determined young man who one day, say in ten years, may shake show business from end to end. For enterprise is his second name.

Consider what happened when he left school at fifteen. He'd never been in a saddle but he loved horses, so off he went to Newmarket to earn five shillings a week training as a jockey. "It wasn't lack of keenness which drove me out of the business," Russ confessed, "but my weight!"

Second to horses, he loved flowers; so the next scene in the Sainty saga shows him as an apprentice in the horticultural department of the Leyton Borough Council, passing exams like mad and winning first prizes with his chrysanthemums.

Next, after his army service, we find Russ with a guitar, a voice, a rock group of his own and no money to put it on the map.

"But that didn't stop us," the future tycoon of Tin Pan Alley recalled "Two of my colleagues and I sold plants from door to door. That way we were able to finance a test record which eventually brought us work with the gramophone companies and the B.B.C."

Next, and this is where our hero differs from so many other aspirants to pop fame, he formed his own little company, with himself as chairman.

"Most singers pay out money to managers and agents," Russ explained, "but we decided to be our own. Now that my records are better known" —a recent one was "Send Me The Pillow That You Dream On" (H.M.V. 45POP1069)—"people keep sending me manuscripts of new songs; some are excellent. So within the next few months we're going into publishing.

"Oh yes—we're moving. The company offices are in my home, but we're going into the West End."

I've told Russ's story in some detail because I feel that here is an utterly new approach on how to get on in pop music. So many young singers, having had a hit or two, sit back and expect the world to come to them. But pop singers come and go

RUSS SAINTY . . .
believes in self-help

alarmingly fast. When one fails, there's always another to take his place.

"By the time the teenagers are tired of me," says Russ, "I'll be doing something different in show business.

Did I mention that Russ, at twenty-five, is unmarried? I don't know his intentions in this matter, but I do know that the girl of his choice will have to move fast to keep up with him!

Jonah Barrington

Woman 22 December 1962

when it came to our work (performing on stage) we took it very seriously and professionally, and we were respected in the business for this. We were always punctual and respectful to both the people booking us and of course our audience, and above all we were always dressed very smartly on stage. We all had our mohair suits made by the famous "Duggie Millings" of Great Pultney Street, London. Duggie was a tailor to the stars, making suits for the likes of Cliff Richard, Adam Faith, The Beatles, Russ Sainty and The Nu-Notes, The Shadows, and the list is endless. I still have a lovely jacket made by Duggie Millings and it still fits me!

Our usual routine during the week would be for Roy Toft, Mel Miller, Roger Dean and myself to meet up at about 10.30am in a small Italian coffee bar, situated in Charing Cross Road. Over a coffee, we would plan our morning, then set off. First we would visit most of the music publishers in Denmark Street (tin pan alley), getting the sheet music of new numbers, then maybe a visit to our agent, Tito Burns, then perhaps a visit to Jennings musical instruments shop and then maybe to Cecil Gees to buy a shirt. After all this we would go back to the Italian coffee bar and many times meet up with a couple of budding songwriters, Mitch Murray and Peter Calender, who were soon to have tremendous success with hits for Gerry and The Pacemakers ("I Like It"and "How Do You Do What You Do To Me?") and for the likes of Paper Lace ("Billy Don't Be a Hero") and plenty more.

We would then all make our own way home by tube train, and then later in the day meet up again for a rehearsal. We usually rehearsed about four afternoons each week. The only reason Bernie our drummer didn't meet up with us each morning was because he lived outside London at Neasden and preferred to just meet up at rehearsals, which sometimes would be at my house in Leyton, East London, or at a small school hall in Stamford Hill, North London. Now as a conclusion to this little bit about us all, I would like to mention that when I first joined The Nu-Notes – Mel Miller, Barry Stoller

(Rhet) and Laurie Joseph (Jay) – they all just happened to be Jewish and I just happened to be Christian. Now after several changes of personnel, a few years later we have Roger Dean, Roy Toft and myself, Christians, and just two Jews, in Mel Miller and Bernie Martin. My point being, whatever combination we have had, it's always been completely harmonious, and for the most part we have all been great friends, and what's more we are still good friends to this day! Why oh why can't religions all around the world be like this, it's so easy? Just be nice to one another. OK Russ, time to get off the soap box.

1962 turned out to be yet another good year for me at the 'Cali'. There were big changes in group personnel. Why? is a question I've asked myself over and over again. Yes, we were working under the name of Russ Sainty and The Rhet Stoller Group, and to be honest, after the initial change from

Fun on the 'Cali' big stage, big Fred the bouncer keeping us all in check, 1962.

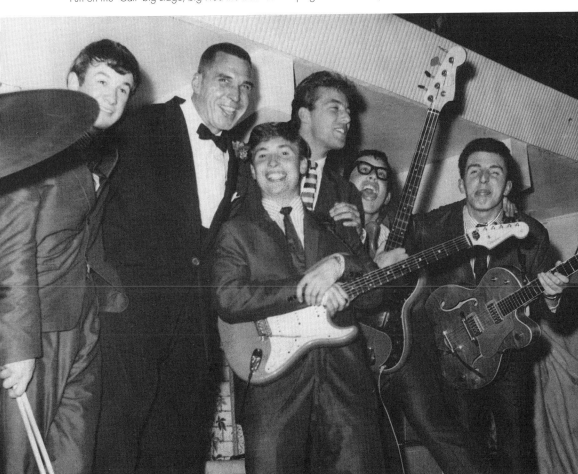

The Nu-Notes, things had gone along very well, but the departure of Rhet and drummer Bernie Martin was quite a shock. The 13th of January being our last performance together. Over the years, I've often given this some thought and my conclusion is this. Though I've no proof that Mr Stoller and Eddy Green, together with Rhet and Bernie, carefully planned the break-up, this line of thought stands up when you see that Rhet Stoller was booked and appeared separately at the 'Cali' on 26th January, just 13 days after our split. Furthermore, in only a matter of a few weeks, Rhet Stoller and The Dynamics were backing many other named artistes, both at the 'Cali' and elsewhere, and guess who was driving them around acting as a "roadie". None other than Mr Green's daughter, Edwina. If my thoughts are correct, and I believe they are, I think this was a naughty thing to do behind my back,

right The only early photo of Edwina Green and myself at the 'Cali', year 1962.
below Autumn 1962, the Office Desk being presented to Russ and the Boys by none other than Mrs Green.

myself having always stood by all the boys in the group, though I had many offers to go as a solo singer. Anyway, it's a long time ago, and I would not want this incident to mar what was a super relationship I had with the Green family. So, after all that, with new group personnel, we become once again Russ Sainty and The Nu-Notes. And that's the way it stayed, right to the end. Wrestling started on 16th January at the 'Cali', and I believe it went very well. I do recall riding round Dunstable on the back of a lorry with a certain Mr Jackie Pallo, wrestler of some repute. This was I believe all in aid of the local carnival and a bit of promotion for the 'Cali'.

It was during the autumn that Mrs Green made me a presentation of an office desk in recognition of my performing well over 200 x 45-minute sets at the 'Cali' – in fact by now I was well on the way to 300, wow! There is no doubt that Mr Green must have had great faith in Russ Sainty and I don't think I ever let him down, though, with his being a shrewd business man, I would have been out before you could shout "Jack Robinson" had I not delivered. People loved me at the 'Cali' and I loved them – it was very, very special. The 7th of September was the last performance at the 'Cali' by Rhet Stoller. I understand that he was finding the pressure of performing just too much and wanted to spend more time recording in his basement studio. Bernie Martin then rejoined The Nu-Notes and Nigel Menday left us for greener pastures – maybe? With Big Jim Sullivan also having left, our group personnel now reads as follows: Russ Sainty (vocals), Mel Miller (bass), Roy Toft (rhythm guitar), Bernie Martin (drums) and Roger Dean (lead guitar), and in all honesty I would say that this line up was probably the best one of all.

Well, as 1962 comes to an end, let's have a wee count up just for the record. OK, I can confirm that this year we did just thirty (30) bookings at the 'Cali', equating to sixty (60) 45-minute sets. A definite drop on the past two years, but fantastic by any standards and yes, I'm still shouting our praises. And this year of 1962 would not be complete without my telling you about Dunstable Young People's Club, at Manchester Place, Dunstable. On Monday 17th September 1962 I had the great pleasure of officially opening this wonderful new Youth Club. This was the culmination of five years' hard work by many notable local Dunstable people, and for me to be asked to open such a Youth Club was indeed a privilege.

What, I wonder, is in store for next year? Please stick with me, because you are about to find out.

right After the presentation, Russ tries out the desk by signing a few autographs,

FRIDAY SEPTEMBER 21 1962

DUNSTABLE BOROUGH GAZETTE

Singer Opens Youth Club's New H.Q.

A LONG-AWAITED and eagerly anticipated event in the lives of Dunstable youth took place on Monday evening, when the new headquarters of Dunstable Young People's Club at Manchester-place was officially opened by popular young local singer, Russ Sainty.

The ceremony on Monday was the climax of more than five years' hard work and effort by many Dunstable people. In his opening speech the Club Chairman Mr. J. J. Gracey outlined the work that had been put into the building. He told how five years ago Cllr. W. T. Lack, who was Mayor at that time, called together representatives from the Pioneer and the Young People's Clubs to discuss the possibility of a joint youth centre. This followed a letter in the "Gazette" from a number of Rotarians concerning the need for such a centre in the Town.

Cllr. Lack then launched an appeal fund to raise money for the premises. The fund was carried on by successive mayors, Cllr. L. Palmer, Ald. P. J. Melton and the present Mayor, Ald. H. Parrott.

"The Fund has received valuable support from the Council and other organisations in the town," said Mr. Gracey, who went on to thank all who had anything to do with the work and also the Ministry of Education and Bedfordshire County Council.

Mr. Gracey mentioned the modern and attractive coffee bar that is one of the main features of the building. The bar has been completely designed and built by members and almost the whole of the construction work was done by member John Combes. Mr. Gracey paid tribute to Mr. Combes, who had put in a lot of very hard work for the Club.

LONG-AWAITED DAY

The Mayor of Dunstable, Ald. Haydn Parrott said that the opening of the new club premises was something that had been long awaited.

He congratulated the Club and paid tribute to the efforts of the public and industrialists of Dunstable who have contributed so much towards the Club. He said he hoped that the Club members would appreciate the work of the management committee who had done such a lot and would do such a lot more in the future.

Looking at the programme that has been arranged for the week, the Mayor said he could see that the emphasis was on variety and judging by this the Club was

obviously going to prosper in the future.

Speaking to the members, he said that the object of the Club was to provide a centre for social and educational activities and to promote a spirit of good citizenship. He emphasised the last part as being very important and said that the Council was anxious that young people should participate as much as possible in the civic life of the town.

Officially opening the premises, Russ Sainty commented on the enormous amount of work that had been done in the past years. He said that in order to make the Club a success work had now got to stop now but had to carry on in the same way.

PRAISE FROM M.P.

M.P. for South Beds, Mr. Norman Cole, described the Club building as a magnificent building. He added that he hoped members would remember that the club was not the building but the fellowship that was in the building.

County Councillor J. Sheffield, who is Chairman of Beds County Council Youth Services Committee, said that he and his committee were trying to see that every place in the County that needed a youth club had one, but he added that he would much rather see a club started and run voluntarily than run by the county.

Mr. A. Hart, Club leader, thanked the visitors for attending and also paid tribute to the Club members for their work. He explained that not only the coffee bar but the coffee tables and the curtains had been the work of Club members. Mr. Hart said that the opening ceremony was a very important night in his life and in the lives of the members.

FOLLOWED BY DANCE

Following the opening ceremony Russ Sainty and his group, The Nu-notes, were the chief attraction at an opening dance at the California Ballroom. Many of the leading figures of Dunstable who had attended the opening, including many councillors and representatives of other organisations in the town, went along to the dance to join in the celebrations.

The dance was the first of a series of social functions to take place during the week.

On Tuesday evening a social and dance was held at the club, the chief attraction being a friendly rock-twist-jive competition. On Wednesday evening the Dunstable Judo Club gave a demonstration and the Bedfordshire county champions gave a demonstration table tennis match. Yesterday was an open club night, when club members were able to see some of the activities in which they will be able to

Singer Russ Sainty, who opened Dunstable Young People's Club on Monday, with some of the canteen helpers.—SR6734.

Russ Sainty turns the key to open the new Dunstable Young People's Club, place, on Monday evening. With him are the Club Chairman, Mr. J. J. Gracey, Leader, Mr. A. Hart.—SR6722.

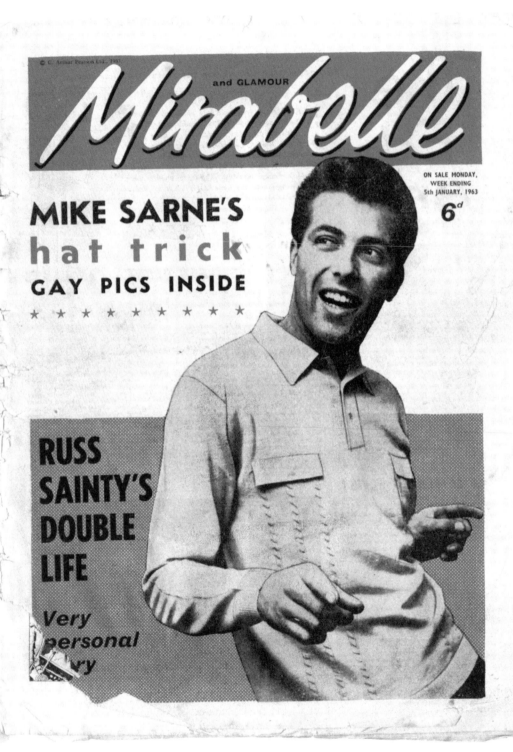

and GLAMOUR

Mirabelle

© C. Arthur Pearson Ltd., 1963

ON SALE MONDAY,
WEEK ENDING
5th JANUARY, 1963

6ᵈ

MIKE SARNE'S
hat trick
GAY PICS INSIDE

★ ★ ★ ★ ★ ★ ★ ★ ★ ★

RUSS
SAINTY'S
DOUBLE
LIFE

*Very
personal
...ry*

Chapter Nine

WITH THE STONES AT THE 'CALI'

Russ Sainty and The Nu-Notes start the New Year of 1963 with plenty of regular bookings from the BBC and the California Ballroom at Dunstable, following the flat spot just before Christmas, forcing us to sell pot plants door to door. I guess that on the strength of our recent tour with Bobby Vee we are also getting bookings coming in from all over the country, including another tour of the Lincolnshire area, where we will once again base ourselves at the Rodney Hotel, Horncastle, owned by Mrs Haigh. From here we shall do most local towns, such as Mablethorpe, Boston, Gainsborough, Skegness, Lincoln City, Louth, Sleaford and many more. The sort of fee we would get for this type of tour would be about £45 per gig and for the solo bookings we could get around £50 to £70, nothing great considering I was on TV, on BBC Radio and making records.

I have to say that despite all the promotion from EMI Records, the Bobby Vee Tour, my TV appearances, my BBC Broadcasts and of course many write-ups in the press, it was now very obvious that my last single, "Send Me the Pillow that you Dream On", was not going to be a hit record for me. OK, it did do very well and was a modest hit, but it was going to be Johnny Tillotson's version that sold the best. I was very disappointed to know that once again my single has failed to make it in the charts. However, it did encourage me to continue writing my own songs, in the hope that I might compose a winner.

Now, on the subject of song writing, I must tell you this little story. I was lucky enough to meet a huge star at this time, Russ Conway. I'm sure some of you will recall his many big hits, played on the old jo-anna – "Side Saddle" and "Roulette" amongst them. I met Russ at an EMI Records promotion party, and we got chatting about us both being a Russ, so he said to me ,"Tell you what we'll do, let's call each other by our real names to make life simple." I said, "OK, that's fine by me, my real name's Alfie, what's yours?" He said, "Terry Stamford, so please call me Terry." Well, we got on really well, and believe me

keeps his own records

LESS than three years ago Russ Sainty was a qualified horticulturalist. In other words, he grew flowers and shrubs for Leyton Town Park near his home.

Today, after spending these years working hard to make a place for himself in showbiz, Russ has proved himself. His latest disc *Send Me the Pillow You Dream On* is being played frequently on radio and TV shows. And there's another one on the way.

But Russ doesn't just perform with his group, and cut discs, he also runs his own business. He is his own manager, publicist and what have you !

And here's some idea of what these jobs mean. ·

Russ works from an upstairs back bedroom at his mother's Leyton home. His "office" is well organised. A chest-of-drawers holds his carefully filed letters and contracts. There are neat piles of headed notepaper, photographs, publicity biographies, in fact, all the documents necessary for self-promotion.

On his large working table is his important diary listing all his working dates. And of course a portable typewriter.

A large map of Great Britain on the wall is dotted with little coloured pins showing where Russ and the Nu Notes have performed, and where all his fans live.

★ ★ ★

Russ is very proud of his fans—and knows how important they are to him. On top of all his other work he has organised a fan club which he runs with a fan club secretary.

"I'm never too busy, or tired to meet my fans," smiled Russ. "I'm so happy to know I have them. You know, sometimes they come here to my home."

"How do you feel about that ? " I asked.

"Oh, I quite enjoy talking to them. I always ask them in and Mum makes them a cup of tea, and we chat and talk about discs. It's easy for them to find me," he grinned.

"Our minibus is always parked outside the house in the road. I painted that sign on it myself," he added, proudly pointing to the "RUSS SAINTY AND THE NU NOTES" sign on the clean green minibus.

"It's great to see the bus so clean. You must do a lot of travelling in it ! " I quizzed.

"The boys help me hose it down and polish it every Saturday. I do all the driving myself. This means I am rarely home before two o'clock a.m."

"But with all the other work you have to do, how do you manage ? "

"I guess it is all a matter of routine, and organisation. Whatever time I get to bed, I'm always at work by nine o'clock. Of course, we have our difficulties, but luckily things have always worked out right in the end."

Russ told me that he had no training for office work at all, and that all the systems he has worked out for his business are his own ideas.

"This business of typing with one finger is a bit annoying," Russ said. "Takes quite a time, but I'm getting better every day. The most annoying thing at present is the telephone."

"What's the difficulty there ? " I asked.

"Trouble is the telephone is downstairs. My office is up. Apart from the danger of breaking our necks and losing weight racing up and down stairs each time it rings. Mum reckons it isn't doing her stair-carpet much good either. But we do have extensions on order, but goodness knows when they will arrive. I'm having a white 'phone for the office," he added.

"It is so frustrating, sometimes I get to the phone just as it stops ringing. Then I spend the rest of the day wondering who it could have been. So if you ever ring and get no reply, give me a chance to get down the stairs ! " (To bring things up-to-date I've just phoned Russ and didn't have to wait a second ! That extension is through and Russ has the phone right under his hand in his office.)

"There are so many stupid things that seem to have happened to me. At first I couldn't realise why the typewriter didn't mark the paper. Then one of the boys pointed out that there wasn't a ribbon in it !

★ ★ ★

"Then there was the time I typed a pile of documents with the carbon paper in the wrong way. And the business of the mixed-up letters. I put the wrong letters in the wrong envelopes."

Although Russ has had his share of teething troubles, he is very serious about the running of his business. He has formed his own company known as R.M.B. Music Limited, in which his group the Nu Notes have shares.

Apart from all the strenuous activities involved in running and performing with the group, Russ still finds time to write songs. He told me he likes to do it late at night when he gets home. He finds it relaxing. This you might think was enough to fill anyone's day, but it isn't !

"Do you have any hobbies, Russ ? " I asked laughingly, sure he hadn't time.

"You know, I like to try my hand at most things. I enjoy interior decorating. I like to cook, and I'm told I'm quite good."

"But I really do like ironing and pressing. I always do my own. I enjoy it."

Did I forget to mention that Russ Sainty is single—Wow ! !

Sylvia Ferguson.

Russ Sainty—the star who works for himself !

17

Mirabelle 5 January 1963

when I say it, he really was a smashing guy, and during conversation we got to talking about songs. Well, this led to Terry (Russ) inviting me to go over to his home, which was at Muswell Hill, North London, because, as he put it, we might be able to compose a smash hit between us. A few days later, I called Russ and went over to see him. We got straight down to songwriting, with Russ trying to find a good melody and me looking for a good title and some lyrics. The outcome of this was a good song, a really big ballad, which Russ (Terry) thought would suit a woman who had been a massive star, Dorothy Squires. Well, a few days later, the song was presented to Miss Squires, and she sang it through and it sounded great. I was so excited and could not believe what was happening. Now, stick with me as I try to explain the outcome. Dorothy Squires was recording for EMI Records under A & R man, Norman Newell, who also had Shirley Bassey, Vera Lynn, Gracie Fields, Noel Coward and The Beverley Sisters, all big stars of their day! Well, if I can put this in a nice way, Mr Newell was also a songwriter, and decided that he would cut me out of this project completely and re-write his own lyrics to our song, making sure that he would get half the

THIS WEEK'S PIN-UP – SHANE FENTON

No. 129—MARCH 16, 1963.
EVERY MONDAY.
5d

Cherie

For Exciting Love Stories in Pictures

THE STORY
OF LOVE AND
A GIRL
CALLED LINDY

SEE PAGES 14 AND 15

March 16, 1963.

CHERIE   23

Debbie, Our Roving Reporter, Quizzes—

RUSS SAINTY

DEBBIE—When and where were you born, Russ?
RUSS—At Leyton, East London, on 13th April, 1938. I've never lived anywhere but at my parents' home.

DEBBIE—Are you using your real name?
RUSS—Sainty is, but I was christened Alfred Charles. When I first sang in a church hall over four years ago some girls nicknamed me Russ and it stuck.

DEBBIE—What did you do when you left school?
RUSS—At 15 my ambition was to be Britain's leading jockey. I started training at Newmarket, became head stableboy and was fired a fortnight later for growing too hefty. I'm almost six feet now and weigh 11 stone.

DEBBIE—Are you in love?
RUSS—With my world! I was very much in love with a girl from Epsom before I entered showbiz. When the professional dates started coming my way and I had to travel, she said I could choose between her and going on the stage. I chose the stage.

DEBBIE—Do you have time for hobbies?
RUSS—Gardening was one, but I've had to let that slide. I love to nip off to the swimming baths in my lunch-hour, and writing songs is a hobby of mine as well as part of my business. Two of mine were, "I've Got A Girl" and "What Do You Know About That?" I'm training hard to read music now.

DEBBIE—You aren't one of the top boys, so how do you account for your tremendous fan following?
RUSS—I guess I'm just lucky, although I do make a fuss of the girls who think something of me. I always write, sign photos, and welcome them. Gsh, they're worth it!

DEBBIE—Is being an East Ender a disadvantage in showbiz?
RUSS—If anything, I believe a tiny advantage. It causes a little laugh and has helped people like Joe Brown, Matt Monro and Lionel Bart. Half the profession is made up of East Enders.

DEBBIE—Have you ever dated a fan?
RUSS—Recently for the first time. E.M.I. ran a competition on my last record, "Send Me The Pillow That You Dream On." The girls had to write in not more than 25 words how they would like to spend the evening with me. Fifteen-year-old Andrea Wood from Gloucester won, out of 1002 entries. She said she wanted us to have a helicopter flight from Battersea down the Thames and back. We had a swell time and finished up at the Pigalle night-club for dinner and dancing.

DEBBIE—Which singers appeal to you most?
RUSS—I like Elvis Presley best, but only in the "pop" field. Then Sinatra and Cliff.

DEBBIE—Do you believe in teenage marriages?
RUSS—No. From what I've seen these seldom work out, because outlook and character can change so much in a few years. I believe one should look around, have a good time before making such a serious decision and then—think twice! Marriage must be for keeps.

DEBBIE—On a date, what's your favourite way to spend an evening?
RUSS—I like to go somewhere quiet, where we can get to know each other properly. Maybe a river trip in the summer and dining out in winter. The shows, films can come later when we feel at ease together.

DEBBIE—Describe your dream girl?
RUSS—Good-looking, about 5 ft. 6 in., with a nice figure and smart. Were I thinking of marriage my girl would have to be able to talk with anyone, know how to behave under any circumstances. I had to learn the hard way, but my dream girl would know instinctively.

DEBBIE—How did you get started in showbiz?
RUSS—I sat in the Two I's coffee-bar in Soho until the manager gave me a chance to sing. Afterwards I sang there for experience, no cash, for six months. I thought if Tommy Steele, Cliff Richard and Eden Kane had all been discovered there, maybe I would have the same good luck. During that time I won a talent competition. Recording managers began to notice me. I was signed for a series of one-night stands and then successfully passed a B.B.C. audition.

DEBBIE—Have you a backing group now?
RUSS—Yes, and they own a slice of me. We've set up a company, RMB Music, Ltd., and the "R," "M," "B" stands for Roy, Melvin and Bernie. We manage ourselves, book our own engagements and all that we earn goes on promotions. We own a typewriter, a telephone, our own notepaper, a filing cabinet and our office is in what used to be my bedroom. A year ago we had a sticky patch so I bought 70 chickens, fattened them up in my office and sold them for enough to keep us going a few weeks. Now our "Do It Yourself" set-up is working out fine.

DEBBIE—You have a fan club, Russ?
RUSS—Oh, sure, and please tell your friends, Debbie, I would be very happy to hear from them. Write—Miss Rosemary Smith, 27 Simonds Road, Leyton, London, E.10.

royalties and not me. Yes, this sort of thing did happen, believe me! I have no idea what the song title was, or whether in fact, the song ever got recorded. As you would expect, having been sort of mugged en route to the recording studio, I lost complete and utter interest in the whole thing. Sadly, Russ Conway died at his Eastbourne home in the year 2000.

It's early 1963, and Ann is now living with her parents, who are managing a small holiday resort on the Isle of Sheppy in Kent. Ann and I are now engaged, having had a small party to celebrate the occasion, though I have to admit that if Ann had not taken some of my dosh and bought the engagement ring herself, it could well have been a year later. I was too wrapped up in my career to even think about things like that, but I'm happy she did! Ann was working in a fashion shop in Victoria, London, which meant her travelling by train from the Isle of Sheppey, getting up at about 5am each morning to achieve this.

As the summer approaches, the Boys and I decide it's now time for a change of transport. For a start, I've made the decision to buy my first car, and with Roy recently having passed his driving test, we decide that he can now take over as the main driver and, just as I've been doing, he can be in charge of the vehicle and use it for himself. However, we think it's time to exchange our green petrol Commer Mini Bus for a new Diesel Commer Bus, which would be cheaper to run and more robust for the hundreds of miles we were clocking up. As for me, well, I'm going to buy myself a brand new Ford Cortina Super 1500cc, colour white, price £675. At just about the same time, my best army mate Tony Edwards from North Weald, Essex, bought himself an MG Midget in red, price about £475 new. Wow! Tony and his new wife Val in their new MG would travel miles to come and see us performing, and I can tell you that on many occasions we would drive flat out on the new MI, which at that

At last! I'm able to buy my first car, a white Ford Cortina Super 1500cc, seen here parked outside the family home in Leyton, with great pride. Year 1963.

time was more or less empty, en route to the 'Cali' at Dunstable. Me in my new white Cortina Super and Tony in his tiny MG Midget, great fun!

I am now desperate to get a new record out as soon as possible, and go to see Walter Ridley at HMV Records, EMI House, Manchester Sq., London. We discuss our failure to get a hit with "The Pillow", and by the tone of Walter's voice it was pretty clear to me that I might not get my contract renewed for another single. However, with our conversation in pessimistic tone, I then asked Walter if he would listen to some new songs and a couple of instrumentals I had recently

An up to date studio shot of myself. Year 1963.

composed. With the group, I had made a demo tape to give some idea of what they would be like. I gave him the tape, which he played and listened to intently, making the odd remark. I just sat there with everything crossed and waited for his final remarks. After about ten minutes, the tape ended, Walter Ridley looked at me and said, "Russ, I think we have something here, I like what I hear. I will have a second listen and call you in a couple of days."

Well, believe me, I went out of his office with a smile from ear to ear, and phoned the boys as soon as I could to tell them the good news. Two weeks later, we are in the Abbey Road Studios and we record two of my own songs, "Unforgettable Love" and "The Twinkle in your Eye", and they both sounded better than anything we had recorded before, in our opinion. EMI Records then got their publicity machine rolling and I was back doing The Friday Night Spectacular for Radio Luxemburg, together with some TV appearances that Tito Burns had lined up, not forgetting our regular broadcasts with the Beeb, and some press coverage in The New Musical Express and The Melody Maker. It seemed that everything was in place for a hit single at last.

To my great surprise, I then get a call from Walter Ridley, telling me he wants to record an instrumental single with The Nu-Notes, and that the numbers will be "Fury", my own composition, and "Hall of Mirrors", composed by Roger Dean (guitar). This was terrific news, made even better by the fact that I had recently formed my own music publishing company, Russanna Music, and

The Nu-Notes larking around whilst having a promotional photo taken for their new instrumental single release, "Hall Of Mirrors", 1963.

would get all the publishing rights on my own material recorded. Wowie! It's all happening. Within a week, we find ourselves back in Abbey Road Studios for the boys to record, and they made a great job of it. All we need now is some luck, and it's possible we could have two hit singles at the same time. However, we are well aware that the Mersey Sound is big, and the Beatles seem to be having hits every other week, not forgetting another group making a big impression, The Rolling Stones. Music trends and sounds were changing; let's hope we are not left behind.

Now, on the subject of The Rolling Stones, who were beginning to make a name for themselves, having already had a record in the hit parade, namely "Come On". They are booked for an appearance at the 'Cali' on July 27th 1963, and will be the support group to Russ Sainty and The Nu-Notes. On the night in question, which I can remember like it was yesterday, Mr Green asked us to go on stage first, simply because The Stones had not yet turned up. Oh dear! Well we did our 45-minute set, and as usual went down really well, and the atmosphere was buzzing, then as we start to leave the stage, bursting through the doors and the very large crowd came several really scruffy guys, carrying sound equipment etc. One of them said to me, "Is it OK to set up around your gear?" to which I replied, "Yes, but don't move anything, we were here set up at 6.30." With that, as they continue setting up their equipment, Eddy Green came up to me and said, "Russ, have you seen the state of these Rolling Stones people?" I said "Yes, what a bloody mess, they are a joke, ha ha." Well, expecting them to follow us into the dressing room (kitchens), I was amazed to see them preparing to start playing, still dressed in the same old filthy clothes in which they arrived. Next, I see Mr Green climb onto the stage and introduce these scruffs. Well, as it turns out, after a couple of numbers the massive crowd surrounding the stage were all eyes transfixed on the lead singer Mick Jagger, who was cavorting his body in a fashion that I for one had never seen. Well, I have to tell you, as you will I'm sure remember if you were there on the night, by the time they had finished their one-hour set, the audience gave the group a tremendous round of applause; they went down fantastic and were indeed the talk of the 'Cali'

It's those handsome lads again, The Nu-Notes, hey, don't scratch my car! 1963.

Another publicity shot of the Boys. Dig those curtains, yes you can have a giggle!

for the rest of that evening. Blimey, it's now our turn to go back on as top of the bill and follow what really was a unique performance by The Stones, scruffy or not! As it turned out, we did finish the night off in style, our loyal fans giving us great support, possibly in sympathy, I shall never know.

What on earth is happening to the pop business, I was thinking, then my feelings were compounded after Eddy Green came over to me and said, "Russ, whatever it is they have got, you need to get some of it." Wise words indeed from a very wise man, and the following Monday at rehearsals The Nu-Notes and myself discussed what action we should take, if any. We decided to cast aside our expensive mohair suits, made by tailor to the stars Duggie Millings, and dress a little more casual, but never, never in the scruffy state of The Stones! It just ain't "Show Biz"!

Russ appears to be trying to frighten the cameraman. Photo taken at the 'Cali', down on the small stage, 1963.

Sitting on the wall of our family home in Leyton are Roger Dean, Roy Toft, our good friend Dave Taberer and Mel Miller. All taking a pit stop whilst cleaning the minibus. Note that Bernie Martin is missing, oh and I'm taking the photo. 1963.

I didn't realize it immediately, but when looking through the forthcoming bookings at the 'Cali', I see that we are once again appearing with The Rolling Stones on 9th August, just a couple of weeks after our first show together. Oh well, this will be interesting, I thought, but as things turned out on this occasion, I believe I'm correct in stating that Eddy Green gave us both equal billing, and on the night we used separate stages to perform our stuff. I have to say this was not such a memorable night, unlike the first one on 27th July 1963.

It's Autumn 1963 and we are still working very hard with plenty of gigs and a bit of TV, promoting our singles, but it was tough going in order to climb those damn charts! Meanwhile, right out of the blue, I am told that two more of my own compositions are about to be released as singles on Oriel Records. They are "Do You Promise" recorded by Bobby Sansom and The Giants, and the other one is "I've Just Had a Letter" recorded by Billy Fontayne. Wow! I just can't believe my luck, that totals five of my own compositions recorded and released as singles in the past couple of months.

Whilst all this is happening, Ann's parents move down to Portsmouth where they will take over the running of a pub called The Hearts of Oak, (sadly no longer there. It's now a ferry port, year 2007). Ann will move down from London and has a new job in Debenhams of Southsea, working in the record department hopefully selling plenty of records by Russ Sainty and The Nu-Notes!

What next? I hear you say. Well, it's sort of good and bad news. I've been seeing a Harley Street specialist about my throat during the past few months and he is getting me into hospital as soon as possible to have my tonsils removed, ouch! However, before I go in, we have a few bookings to complete around the Midlands and Derbyshire areas and we book into a small hotel in Ashby-de-la-Zouch, (sounds like a foreign country). Our last gig of the week was the Co-op Hall in Swadlincote and our support group were called The Fortunes. I will never forget that night, after their manager Reg Calvert took me to one side and told me that his group The Fortunes were brilliant and would put us in our place. I found this a strange thing to come out with, but I admit they were very good, but no, they didn't put Russ Sainty and The Nu-Notes in their place.

Well, after the show, I was hurriedly driven to the nearest railway station

It's autumn 1963, Russ Sainty and The Nu-Notes in action at a gig in Swindon.

1963, Russ in full flow at another charity bowls competition; in the background Mel Miller looks on.

and got a train back to London. Why? Well, I had to be admitted into the Homeopathic Hospital near Tottenham Court Road, London on the Monday morning for my anxiously awaited tonsil op. Now, during the past few weeks, I have negotiated a month's booking for The Nu-Notes in Hamburg, Germany. This will help them to keep a few pennies coming in whilst I am out of action. It will be quite a while before I can sing again; in fact I've been told that I will not be allowed to even talk for at least a month following my operation. Some might say that's a good thing! In truth at 27 years old, it's not the most pleasant of small ops. Though I have to say it all went well and after about a week I was well on the mend, but silent!

It was not easy communicating, but after a while Ann and I devised a simple method. When she called me on the phone, she would ask all the questions and I would answer with one tap for yes and two taps for no, simple really, but very, very boring after a month.

The Boys made contact and it was clear that they were doing OK in Hamburg, but to our great disappointment, our singles were not climbing the Hit Parade as we had hoped. Yes, they were selling, but unfortunately not enough to make the top twenty charts. Will we get any more chances to record? That is what is worrying me, but I am going to keep composing new songs, I'M NOT DONE YET!

It's about November 1963 and the Boys return from Hamburg, and I am now able to talk and want to get rehearsing again to see how my throat is shaping up, and whether or not it has affected my singing voice. I call a rehearsal at my house in Leyton, which was the first time I had seen the Boys since their return. It was a strange meeting; something was not the same between us. Remember, I was quite a bit older than all of them and had always taken care of all the business side of things; bookings, the fan club and all the driving until recently, so you can imagine how I was feeling, in a word, hurt. Even more so when you consider I had always split our fees five ways. I had never ever taken a penny more than anyone else, and what's more, it was with my help and initiative that they had had a month's work abroad anyway. We had a sort of rehearsal that afternoon and I was happy that my voice was doing fine with no sore throat, but on our departure that day, we did exchange a few words and I told them exactly what I thought of them. Roy Toft came back at me, saying how well they had done in Germany and what they had lined up for their future, etc., etc., and in a few words said that The Nu-Notes didn't need Russ Sainty anymore. I must be honest; I was shocked, disgusted, let down and as I said before, very hurt! However, we agreed to do the bookings together that were already under contract, one

Russ in relaxed mood with a friend's horse, "Marla". At 15 years old, Russ was an apprentice jockey based at Newmarket.

of which was at the Leyton Swimming Baths, date 22nd November 1963. We had performed for our first 45-minute spot when somebody rushed in to say President Kennedy had been assassinated. We all stopped and looked at each other in complete disbelief and asked the question, "Are you certain of this?" and we were told once again, "Yes, it's true, it's true." Well, if nothing else it sure took the steam out of our performance, which wasn't going with too much enthusiasm anyway.

Having completed all our contractual gigs, we split and I didn't see or hear from the Boys for a few weeks, not having any idea what work they were going to do. As for myself, well I had my regular BBC bookings and I was still doing a bit of photographic modelling work and of course I was still composing new songs, so I was keeping busy. Problem for me was that Tito Burns was still filling our calendar with new bookings as I hadn't told him about the split. Fortunately, this all played right into my hands, because within a few weeks I get a call from Roy (Nu-Notes) and he wants to talk to me and it turns out that the group has had no bookings; all the promises to them had fallen through and in a word, they were desperate.

After a short discussion with Roy, I agreed to work with The Nu-Notes, just as before, but the difference this time would be financial. I was now about to employ the Boys for £7 per gig and I would pay a small contribution towards fuel, depending on the mileage, and travel with the Boys in the bus just as we had always done before. Roy agreed to this and in my opinion, he was grabbing this offer with two hands. Yes indeed, the tables had turned and the Boys had brought it all on themselves, he said very smugly. For me, it meant I could make anything between £40 and £55 per show and for the first time since I started singing in 1957 would make some good money. Incidentally, the BBC at this time were paying me £12 per show. Sounds a bit pathetic now, but it wasn't too bad in those days. As 1963 comes to an end, Russ Sainty has plenty to think about if he is to keep at the top of the pile in this now very competitive pop business.

This year of 1963 has definitely been very eventful for Russ Sainty and The Nu-Notes, and we would also see our favourite venue, the California Ballroom, now attracting some of the biggest names in pop, people like Eden Kane, Johnny Kidd, The Hollies, Marty Wilde, The Swinging Blue Jeans, The Searchers, Gerry and The Pacemakers, Cliff Bennett, Vince Eager and American acts like The Eagles, Gene Pitney, Gene Vincent, Johnny Burnette, and many more. It's quite clear that the 'Cali' is the place to be seen, without doubt. However, I have to tell it as it is, and I can confirm that despite all the big guns appearing week after week, bookings for Russ Sainty and The Nu-

Notes continued to be good, and although I missed a couple of months whilst having my tonsils removed and The Nu-Notes were in Germany for about six weeks, we still notched up seventeen (17) bookings, equating to thirty-four (34) x 45-minute sets, which I'm happy to say was more than any other artist by far, and has been the case for the past three years now!

Will things at the 'Cali' continue for us in the same way next year? Only time will tell!

A studio shot of Russ, 1963.

January 25, 1964. Every Thursday 6d

Jackie
for go-ahead teens

FREE 30 DAY BEAUTY COURSE
A handy book for a lovelier you

THE LOVES AND HATES — of Russ Sainty

Here's a fella who really enjoys running his own fan club—and the membership figures show that the personal touch counts! That's Russ Sainty—the boy who takes the trouble! And here are the things that Russ digs—or digs a grave for . . .

I LOVE

hearing church bells, especially when bell ringers are at work. Often stand listening outside St Paul's.

feminine girls in floating chiffon with soft sweeping hair.

sitting in a steamy bath around 2 a.m. thinking up songs.

Presley.

riding and talking to horses, p'raps because I'm an ex-jockey.

driving big, fast cars. I've got a white Cortina, but with more lolly I'd like an E-type Jaguar

answering fan club letters. I run my own fan club and answer all letters personally —my record was 301 in a week!

running around Leyton Park before breakfast.

modelling, but active—on a yacht, up a ladder.

I LOVE all London parks because I'm a real Cockney, born within sight and sound of Bow Bells. This to me is countryside.

I HATE going to a barber. But if they were all like this girl, it'd be all right!

I HATE

gooey sweets after a meal. Why spoil good food?

to see girls smoking in the street.

coming home late at night when folks are asleep. Horrible empty, quiet, cold feeling

those mods who wear skirts well below the knee

people who run me down because I'm a pop singer and don't take the trouble to get to know me.

characters who grab me and say "Gimme a photo, gimme an autograph" with never a please.

parsnips, though my Mum and Dad love them.

a "date" who is completely tongue-tied. I'm shy, too!

gin. Makes my inside turn over

Chapter Ten

MATCH OF THE DAY

Beatlemania and The Mersey Sound are still here, London is still swinging and Carnaby Street the place to shop! Mods and Rockers fight on Brighton Beach, Cassius Clay beats Sonny Liston to become World Heavyweight Champion, 28th March, and Radio Caroline Pirate Radio is on air! Match of the Day on TV, and 1st January 1964 new on TV, "Top of the Pops". Elvis, Cliff and The Shadows continue with hit records.

Meanwhile, Russ Sainty loses his contract with EMI, HMV Records because once again my latest single has failed to make the hit parade. I felt sure that my recording of "Unforgettable Love" would make the charts; it's a good record and I'm completely baffled as to why I do so well in live performance but cannot get into the charts. Oh well, I've just got to try harder and keep writing songs in the hope I will get a winner! Thankfully, we are still very busy as a group and I continue to get some photographic modelling work and BBC Broadcasts, and I get a fair share of press coverage, including those teenage girlie mags, Mirabelle and Cherie, where I've been lucky enough to have been on front covers, back covers and inside stories. Now, you may be wondering what happened to Rhet Stoller since leaving The Nu-Notes and the break-up about six months ago of his new group The Dynamics. Well I can confirm that Rhet has built a recording studio in the basement of his parents' house at Stamford Hill and he's recording some good stuff, all by multi-track method, meaning he uses two recording machines and records, let's say, the bass line, after which he will over dub, say, rhythm guitar, followed by an over dub (recording) of, say, lead guitar and so on and on and on until he builds up a completed recording. It just happened that Rhet's cousin was going out with a sports writer called Sam Leach and, after listening to some of Rhet's work, he asked him if he could write and produce a tune for a new television show to be screened later that year. It was a football show called Match of the Day! Well, the rest is history, as the saying goes. Rhet composed, played and tracked almost every part on the Match of the Day theme, including the drums. A truly great tune of which he played and recorded almost every part, an outstanding achievement that turned out to be a world hit and is still being played all over the world to this day. Rhet did much the same with many other great compositions and he did put out a couple of albums, most of which I still have to this day. I was in close contact with Rhet at this time and I too was very busy composing new songs, of which we would sometimes make demos together in his small studio. We also composed together one song which was called "How Can I Tell Maureen" and was recorded by The Hamilton Folk 4 on Columbia Records in 1965.

Early summer of '64, I was on Southsea Common with Ann one Sunday afternoon and a new song came into my head and within half an hour I had composed the whole thing from start to finish. On the following Monday at our usual rehearsals in my parents' house in Simonds Rd., Leyton, I sang it over to the Boys, who then put an arrangement around it and we all agreed it sounded good. It was called "That's How I'm Gonna Love You". I had by now composed at least a dozen new songs of which we had recorded demos. Question was, are any of them good enough to get to the top? From my days at the 2 i's Coffee Bar, I had always been inspired by the great Elvis Presley and Ricky Nelson, and I decided that the next time I went into a recording studio I was going to record one of Ricky's old hits called "Lonesome Town". It had always been one of my favourites and I felt it could be a hit all over again. I was told about a small but good recording studio south of Tottenham Court Road tube station, so set out one morning to find the place. I can't remember the name of the studio, but the fellow who was running the place was also the recording engineer and after a short meeting both he and I had made a deal and a date to record a couple of songs, just to see what we could produce together. Once again, I cannot recall his name. A few days after our meeting we arrived at the studio and firstly recorded "Lonesome Town", followed by my own composition, "That's How I'm Gonna Love You". The session went well and we all agreed that "Lonesome Town" was good enough to be released as a single 45 record, but of course I didn't have a contract. I decided to take a copy of the two songs to a good friend who just happened to be Norrie Paramour's assistant at EMI's Columbia Label. Off I go to a familiar stamping ground, EMI House, Manchester Square, London, but this time to a different office, only yards away from my last recording manager, Walter Ridley. Well, I handed over my tape to Bob Barrett, who played it all through after which he said, "I like it Russ, can I keep it and let Norrie hear it tomorrow?" To which I was delighted to say, "Yes mate, thanks very much." A few days later,

I was back in his office and doing a financial deal for Parlophone Records, an off shoot of EMI Columbia label to lease the recordings from me and release them as a new single, with "Lonesome Town" as an A side and my own song, "That's How I'm Gonna Love You" on the B side. I just could not believe it. At my first attempt I've recorded and produced my own single, good enough to be leased by the great EMI Ltd., with all costs of the vinyl production and distribution of the single down to them. Well, once again the publicity machine at EMI was in action and I was recording shows for Radio Luxemburg, doing my regular BBC Broadcasts, and my agent lined up some telly. Whilst all this was happening, Walter Ridley called me to say that following their last record, which did quite well, he would like to do another one with The Nu-Notes on his HMV label. It seems that he had dug up a demo

RUSS

Secretary : Rosemary Smith
59 Chelsea Green, Linslade, Leighton Buzzard, Beds.

Date

SAINTY Fan Club

NEWSLETTER NO. 19.
July,
AUGUST & SEPTEMBER
19 64.

(Incorporating 'THE NU-NOTES')

Well Hallo again everybody,

Its sure good to be writing to you all once again and may I say first of all that we all at the Club sincerely hope you are all "fit and well", and a big Hallo to our New Club Members, its great to have you with us.

Looking out of our office window, I can see the Sun shining (for a change) which reminds me that many of you have had or are having your holiday's and I guess many of you are looking forward to going? Well which ever it is, we hope you have all been able to listen in to Russ and the Nu-Notes on Evergreen each Monday night at 10.0 pm. We know a lot of you have by the nice letters you have sent to the B.B.C. and to us, for which Russ is very pleased and asked me to say Tar :! for him.

During the past Month or so Russ and himself has been writing a lot of new songs. The reason for all the Boy's have been very busy doing recording sessions and Russ this?? Well many reasons, but one special one and that is this- Russ has at long last made a NEW RECORD and we are sure you'll agree that its about time too. I won't tell you much about it now but we will be sending you all a special letter very soon. But what I can tell you is that Russ wrote the song on the "flip" side of the record and its a real good one. Also more good news, Russ has recently joined Norrie Paramour of Columbia Records, who is Cliff and the Shadows recording manager and of course many other well known stars. This is great news because already they are making plan's for recording many new songs for future release.

Well before I close this page, as always, may I say on behalf of all at this end, if any of you are poorly we wish you a very very speedy recovery, GET WELL SOON.
Yours Saintly,
Brehda & Rosemary.

Hon. Members : TOMMY STEELE, BILLY FURY, EDEN KANE, BOBBY VEE
THE CRICKETS, SHANE FENTON, THE FENTONES and DANNY WILLIAMS

RUSS WRITES FOR Y O U
TO Y O U.

So grab! your glasses and eye's down (no its not bingo) Ha, ha. As alway's its my pleasure to be back on the key's and being in contact with you all. Of course its very possible that you won't even get this letter owing to a certain Post offoce affair, O.K. enough said in case your Dad is a post man.

Well friends as the girls have told you, its only a few weeks and I will have a new record out for you, it will be next Month sometime but we will let you know the date in a special letter. Bytheway, have any of you bought KATHY the NU-NOTES latest record ? Personally I think its a real smashing record at least its different and a great tune, of which Mad Mel wrote. Anyway I hope you may like it and give a request now and then.

Hey guess what? Well since our last letter, Roger The Groups guitarist has left and his place has been taken by our old guitarist Rhet Stoller, so now the group is back to its original members. As we mentioned before I do work apart from the group. now and at present am trying to do a deal with a film company, but I'll tell you more about that in my next letter. One thing for certain, that is that I have just formed a New Publishing Company so if any of you or your friends fancy your selfs as song-writers, then nows your chance, because all you need do is to sing it on a tap and send it to:-27, Simonds RD., Leyton, London, E.IO. and I will see what can be done for you, if the songs are good you to can make a fortune like the Beatles.

Oh bytheway, in my last letter I said that I was or maybe going to the Channel Isle's, well I did'nt go. It would have ment to much traverling because as you well know, we have to be in London for our weekly Broadcast on "EVERGREEN". Say do you like the idea of me doing a couple of old million sellers each week? I hope so, at least we try to add a little interest to the programme.

I short time ago I mentioned pen friends, well Ive an address of a girl in Africa who wants someone to write to, the name is Francis Anigyei Darko,
P.O. Box 39, R/C Middle School,
Akwatia, GHANA, West Africa.
Now let me think to see if ive not told you all that I should have done---I can't think of any thing that Ive missed except to say, as alway's, Be Good---Be Happy--- and most of all Keep Healthy.
P.S. Our little dog is getting on just great, and the Cortina is going like a rocket! !
Bye for now,
Yours alway's,
sincerely Russ.

An example of the Russ Sainty Fan Club letter dated 1964, oh happy days!

tape we had given him a few months previously, which had on it, amongst others, a new instrumental composition by our bass player and funny man, Mel Miller. Mr Ridley gave the Boys a one record deal (contract) and they went into those now famous Abbey Rd. Studios once more and the recording was done in a three-hour session. The A side was to be Mel's composition "Kathy" and on the B side an oldie called "Sunset". Walter Ridley decided that the beautiful acoustic guitar playing of Roger Dean would sound even better if accompanied by a big string orchestra, and he was right. It is in my opinion a beautiful sound and confirmed just how good The Nu-Notes were. OK, we now have two records on the market and we do everything possible to promote them. However, just as before, The Nu-Notes don't get any television. It's so damn annoying, they deserve better. We are furious about this and just don't know why. Oh well, lets keep working away and perhaps our luck will change. Thankfully, we have plenty of gigs all over the country including our regular Cali Ballroom bookings. At home, Derek Day is still running my little office in my mum's upstairs back room, 27 Simonds Rd., Leyton, and my parents and sister are all OK. Ann and I have decided to get married next March, which is still a long way off, but I haven't yet told Mum and Dad!

As the weeks go by, though we are getting plenty of plays on BBC and Radio Luxemburg, it's pretty clear that once again we are not going to make the charts and Top Twenty with either my single or The Nu-Notes' single. Yes, we are selling records but simply not enough. At our next rehearsal, we have a chat about things, and I suggest we all go away for a two-week package holiday to Majorca. Our depression about failing records was compounded by the fact that some old friends, who were our supporting group for a couple of years in the late fifties, called The Dave Clark Five, have recently had a number one smash hit record with "Glad All Over" and, like my last record, the boys did it independently – perhaps we have started a new trend? With regard to the holiday, well it finished up that only Roy and myself wanted to go, so I booked for two weeks in a place called Paguara in Majorca, the cost for two weeks' half board was about £35 each. Of course, this type of holiday in 1964 was fairly new, but very quickly caught on, and is now the norm, just a bit more expensive. Ha Ha. I have to say, our holiday turned out to be fabulous, but like all good things, it had to come to an end. On our return, I get some good news – Bob Barrett at Columbia Records is about to record one of my own compositions called "Tell the Other Guy", and the singer is a successful Australian by the name of Brian Davis. I have to say, Brian did a great job with my song, and though not a big hit it did sell pretty

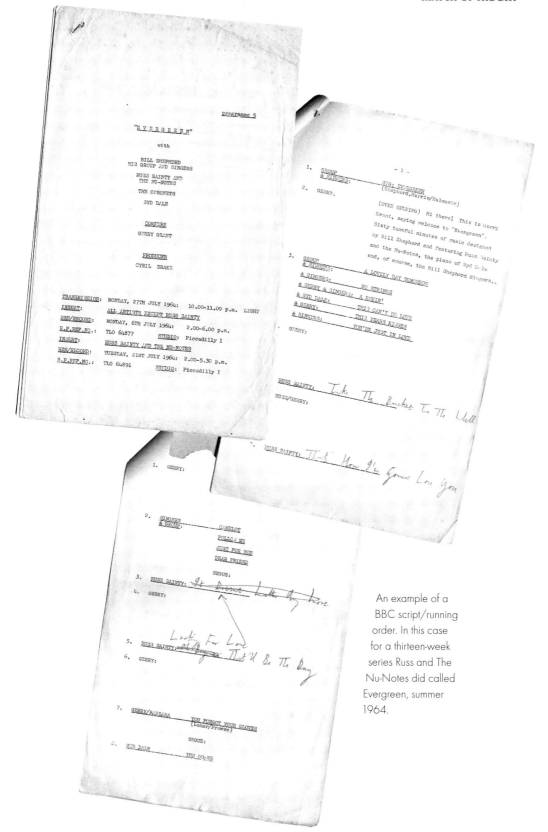

Programme 5

"E V E R G R E E N"

with

BILL SHEPHERD
HIS GROUP AND SINGERS

RUSS SAINTY AND
THE NU-NOTES

THE CORONETS

SYD DALE

COMPERE
GERRY GRANT

PRODUCER
CYRIL DRAKE

TRANSMISSION: MONDAY, 27TH JULY 1964: 10.00-11.00 p.m. LIGHT
INSERT: ALL ARTISTS EXCEPT RUSS SAINTY
REH/RECORD: MONDAY, 6TH JULY 1964: 2.00-6.00 p.m.
R.P.REF.NO.: TLO 64877 STUDIO: Piccadilly I
INSERT: RUSS SAINTY AND THE NU-NOTES
REH/RECORD: TUESDAY, 21ST JULY 1964: 2.00-5.30 p.m.
R.P.REF.NO.: TLO 64891 STUDIO: Piccadilly I

1. GROUP   - 1 -
   & SINGERS: SIG: EVERGREEN
                       (Shepherd, Harris/Halmusic)
2. GERRY:
                       (OVER OPENING) Hi there! This is Gerry
                       Grant, saying welcome to "Evergreen",
                       Sixty tuneful minutes of music designed
                       by Bill Shepherd and featuring Russ Sainty
                       and the Nu-Notes, the piano of Syd Dale
3. GROUP   and, of course, the Bill Shepherd Singers..
   & SINGERS: A LOVELY DAY TOMORROW
   & SINGERS: NO STRINGS
   & GERRY & SINGERS: A ROVIN'
   & SYD DALE: THIS CAN'T BE LOVE
   & GERRY: THIS YEARS KISSES
   & SINGERS: YOU'RE JUST IN LOVE
   GERRY:

RUSS SAINTY: Take The Bucket To The Well

RUSS/GERRY:

7. RUSS SAINTY: That's How I'm Gonna Love You

1. GERRY:

2. SINGERS
   & GROUP: CAMELOT
                      FOLLOW ME
                      JUST FOR YOU
                      DEAR FRIEND
                      SEGUE:
3. RUSS SAINTY: It Doesn't bother my love
4. GERRY:

5. RUSS SAINTY: Looking For Love   That'll Be The Day
6. GERRY:

7. GERRY/BARBARA   YOU FORGOT YOUR GLOVES
                      (Lehar/Frowse)
                      SEGUE:
8. SYD DALE   THE OO-BE

An example of a
BBC script/running
order. In this case
for a thirteen-week
series Russ and The
Nu-Notes did called
Evergreen, summer
1964.

well, both home and abroad, and yes, I did make a few quid on royalties!

Meanwhile, I'm still without a record contract; remember my last single was recorded independently as a one off. Question is, can I get out of jail once again and find a way to get another single on the market? Well, surprise surprise! We are travelling to a gig in Suffolk, a place called Aldeburgh and I came up with an old song which I thought we could do, perhaps in a similar style to what The Bachelors had done with "Diane" and "Charmaine". I sang it over to the boys and within half an hour we had a complete arrangement for the song, including vocal harmonies. We all get quite excited and wonder could this be the one to put us in the charts? I can hear you saying, "OK Russ, what's it called?" Let me tell you, the song is an oldie called "This is my Lovely Day". The gig went well and I recall we did a bit of scrumping on the way home, clambering through a big hedge and into an orchard, nicking apples, great fun, but naughty at our ages. A couple of days later, we went into a small studio in Denmark Street and recorded a demo of the song, together with a new composition I had just written, called "Bless You Girl". Wasting no time at all, I then went straight up to see my old pal Bob Barrett at Columbia Records EMI House, where we played the demo tape for Bob's approval. Without hesitation, Bob flipped! "Yes," he said, "I think both songs are very good and I'm going to offer you a two record contract." Once again I was in business, and telephoned the Boys to tell them of my good news. Now, I guess by now you, my dear reader, are finding this all a bit monotonous, with one record deal following another. What else can I do, but tell you things as they were? Please hang on in with me, as it's not too long now before things change in a big way.

Russ Sainty and The Nu-Notes are back once again in Abbey Road Studios. By now we are getting to know the place very well. We have recorded in studios No.1, 2 and 3, but as yet we have not recorded a winner. Optimistically, I feel sure this is the one, and for whatever reason, I can't remember, but Rhet Stoller is playing lead guitar for us in place of Roger Dean – perhaps he was sick? As was usual with Rhet, he found some nice guitar parts for both songs, in particular for my song "Bless You Girl". The recording went well and we now await the release date of yet another single! Once again, EMI Records get the publicity machine rolling and it is a repeat of everything I've done before, only difference being I no longer have Tito Burns as my sole agent. Instead, I will now get work from any agent who wishes to book us out. Well, a week or so goes by and my new single is released. We were quite busy and thankfully we were still doing fairly regular BBC Broadcasts, but I cannot recall getting any television to help promote this single. Oh well, let's just do the best we can and hope the single starts to move. Meanwhile Ann is still living at her parents' pub in Portsmouth, the Hearts of Oak, and we are now making serious plans for our wedding next March. I get round to telling Mum and Dad, who didn't make a lot of comment, but I would have to say they didn't get excited and congratulate me! We decided to have our wedding at the Cathedral Church of St. Thomas of Canterbury, known as Portsmouth Cathedral, in Old Portsmouth, and we went to see the Canon, who would be the person to take our marriage service, to make sure we had the date 6th March 1965 well and truly booked.

As the weeks go by, you may well have guessed that my latest single is only moving slowly, and it would be fair to say it was not going to be a hit! I'm quite sure that by now you are feeling as frustrated as I was at the time. Not only frustration – I had all sorts of emotions and questions that I needed someone to answer as to why I continued to fail with my records. So many people had faith in me, as you can see by the amount of times I continually had the opportunity to make yet another new single. Was it bad luck, perhaps the songs were not good enough, is it because I manage myself, am I promoting the records properly? So many questions, but I don't know the answers. However, very soon, I will reveal some relevant information that even now on occasions makes me cry.

So what of 1964 for Russ Sainty and The Nu-Notes at the California Ballroom? As you can see, we have been very busy, but for one reason or another our bookings at the 'Cali' have dropped off considerably and to be very honest, there is nothing memorable for me to report, except to say that once again, for the year 1964 we did get booked more than any other artiste! Yes, it was in fact just six (6) bookings, equating to twelve (12) 45-minute sets. So now for the past five (5) years on the trot Russ Sainty has been booked more than anyone else. Yippie, I am so proud of these figures, which until writing my memories of the 'Cali' I really didn't know were fact. Sorry if I'm getting excited, but as I mentioned earlier in my story, at my age now I'm gonna shout my achievements with dignity and pride!

Next year is almost upon us, and will see big changes.

Chapter Eleven

FAREWELL TO THE 'CALI' AND THE NO. 1 DREAM

The Rolling Stones have three number one hits, Tom Jones, Donovan, Cilla Black, Sandie Shaw, Dusty Springfield and of course The Beatles churn out the hits. Flower Power and the first hippies, Anti Vietnam War Demonstrations and once again, Russ Sainty is without a recording contract.

Work for Russ and the group is slowing down and, to be honest, we were all feeling a bit incomplete as a group. Here we are around seven years on since we first performed as Russ Sainty and The Nu-Notes, we have been there and done it all as a pop group, but sadly both The Nu-Notes and myself have failed miserably to get into the Top Twenty charts, which really is the all important thing, as of course it still is to this day. It's a kind of yardstick which you are measured by, it's what gets you on all the TV shows and chat shows, you are without doubt judged by both the public and the industry by the success or lack of it when it comes to hit records. Question is, will we or I get any more chances? We shall have to wait and see. I for one will not give up trying. As March 6th draws ever closer, I now concentrate on my marriage and we booked our honeymoon in The Omerooh Hotel, Jersey. I must have been very nervous and anxious as I left home in Leyton on the afternoon of 5th March. More so because I knew Mum was upset and I wanted this to be a time of great happiness for everyone. That night I stayed with Pat and Stan Filtness at a Pub called Union Tavern in Old Portsmouth. I didn't sleep too well, as you would expect, and before I could even think straight, it was time to head off to the Cathedral. It was only a few minutes away and on my arrival I could see crowds of people, some I knew and most I didn't know. Neither did I expect Southern Television cameras to be there, or lots of press photographers and reporters. It was very obvious that, even though we had tried to keep the whole thing very quiet, somebody had

As the Cathedral bells chime, Russ and Ann Sainty make their way to a waiting limo. Job done!

informed the media. Oh well, it's too late now, so let's get on with things. I walk up the aisle and say hello to my parents and other family members. I also spot my best man, Tony Edwards, remember him? My best mate in the Army. We had a chat and then took up positions to await my bride. Now, I don't intend going through all the details of the service, after all a wedding is a wedding and I can't remember much about it. I think I was on auto pilot. Everything went well, we did all the photos, and the press had fun taking their pics. Confetti was everywhere, but it seemed like in a flash we had left the Cathedral and arrived back at the Hearts of Oak pub, where we had our reception. It was a long day, and lots of people were going to stay all night, sleeping wherever they could find a cosy corner or one of the many beds that had been prepared and made available. Apart from an aunt and uncle on my side of the family, complaining that they had been promised a double bed, everyone else just muddled in and got their head down wherever they could. Ann and myself had booked into a hotel in Southsea for the night and would get a flight to Jersey the next day from, believe it or not, Portsmouth Airport (now a housing estate). The flight was quite an experience We flew in an old Dakota aircraft, very rickety and a bit shaky, but we arrived in Jersey where we spent a few memorable days. We were not able to stay for a full week due to the fact that I had a BBC broadcast to do.

We had provisionally rented a flat in Clapton, just a few miles from my parents in Leyton. I had put down a deposit many months previously on a three bedroom new house at Cheshunt, Hertfordshire (Cliff Richard's old home town) and we were waiting for the house to be completed, which I was told might be at least another ten months. We settled into the flat alright and Ann got herself a temporary job in the office of a big garage about ten minutes away in Lea Bridge Rd., Leyton, E10. Meanwhile, it was only a few minutes drive for me to get to meet the group for rehearsals at Stamford Hill. However, though we still had a few bookings in the diary, it was getting harder and harder for Russ Sainty and The Nu-Notes to get work. Also, I could sense a kind of apathy and a definite lack of interest, something that was a sort of hangover after our last record failed to make it, and of course my getting married might have something to do with it. I decide to call a meeting with all the Boys and find out just how everyone felt. It was not our usual jovial banter, something was different and I wanted some answers. I asked the Boys one by one just what their feelings were. Mel, Roy, Bernie and Roger all came up with the same answer, "Russ, we think its all over; we have all chatted together about this and feel that the time is right for us to call it a day and put an end to Russ Sainty and The Nu-Notes as a unit." My

Its March 6th 1965, Russ and his girlfriend Ann Graham finally tie the knot and get married at Portsmouth Cathedral. Photo showing both sets of parents, with the two bridesmaids on the flanks.

reply was simple, "Fellows, very sadly I have to agree with you all, it feels that this is the end of the road and has been coming for some time." I asked the Boys, "Have you got anything lined up? Where will you go from here?" Well, I can confirm that after a while Roger Dean (lead guitar) joined various other groups and is still doing the same thing to this day, but he also teaches guitar as a more reliable living. Roy Toft (rhythm guitar) first became a driving instructor and later moved to Kingston upon Thames, where he became a bus driver, but then progressed to become an inspector for the bus company. Bernie Martin (drums) went to Italy to join a group called The Bad Boys, who had several number one hits and were a very successful group, something The Nu-Notes were not able to achieve. Mel Miller (bass guitar) worked the markets for a while, but soon got into the property business and had his first hotel in London's Kings Cross, followed by another in my old home territory, Leytonstone, East London.

But fellows, first we have one more gig to do and it's very fitting that this will be our last show together; it's the California Ballroom on April 24th. I have a chat with the Boys and ask them to really try and pick themselves up, because I want us to go out with a bang, as the saying goes. Well, they didn't let me down; we all performed at our best, and yes, I think we did go out with a bang! And in style, showing our class and professionalism.

Thankfully, I still had my BBC work, together with some model and advertising photographic work, but I needed to sort out my life with regard to singing. I decided to put a cabaret act together, which was completely different to what I had been doing with the group. For a start, I would need to choose the correct type of songs, some with a bit of sophistication perhaps. I needed a good opening and a very strong finish to the act. Furthermore, I had to get someone to write up all the sheet music. Meanwhile, I get a call from my old pal at EMI Columbia Records, Bob Barratt, who asked if I was up for a bit of session work in the recording studios. I jumped at the opportunity and went straight up to Manchester Square to see him. Bob explained that he had composed a lot of new songs and would like me to record them in order that he would then have demo records to be able to play to various artistes, in the hope they would record them for the general market place. This is the normal practice for any song writer who needs to get his or her work recorded. Well, we routined about a dozen songs and I went into a small London studio with a four or sometimes five-piece band, led by a great keyboard player, Mr Harry Stoneham, who in more recent years played for Parkinson on TV. As it happens, doing this demo work for Bob not only brought in some cash, it was to benefit me in the future, quite unexpectedly.

During these demo recording sessions I played Bob a couple of my new songs, one of which he liked very much but thought he could improve the lyrics. We got together one early evening in his office and between us we completed the song, Bob having changed some of the words, and it sounded good! Bob said to me, "Russ, I know you haven't got a contract with us (Columbia Records) at present and I'm not sure I can get a new one for you after your recent failures, but if I find another decent song I will see what I can do." Wowie, I just can't believe it, am I going to get another chance to make a new single?

A couple of weeks later, around about May/June time, Bob contacted me and said he was sending me a demo of an American song and to let him know what I thought of it. The post arrived and both Ann and myself played the

Russ, now a married man, continues with his photographic modelling work. summer 1965.

Russ Sainty

left The photo that secured me a two-week advertising job in Spain. The results of which later went on all the big advertising hoardings around the UK.

demo, with all fingers crossed – please let it be good! A few minutes later, having played the demo twice over, we both agreed it was a very good song. I try singing it over in the hope it suits my voice and range; Ann is busy writing down the words, and all in all we were both quite excited. I called Bob and told him what we both thought and he seemed pleased that I liked the song, and said to leave things with him and he will get back to me. The song was called "She", no, not the one sung by that Frenchman, Charles Aznavour, and the song I had composed with Bob was called "Saving My Tears (For a Rainy Day)". A week later, Bob contacts me and wants me to meet him in his office. When I get there, he introduces me to Ivor Raymond and tells me, "Russ, I've persuaded the powers-that-be to give you a new two record contract and we will have Ivor Raymond do the orchestral arrangements for these two songs. Furthermore, I've booked No.2 studio at Abbey Road." Well, I was just blown away. I cannot believe what is happening. I thought my recording days were over. The big day comes; I make my way to the studio and get there in good time, feeling just a bit anxious, then as I walked into studio 2 I was stopped in my tracks. In front of me was a 35-piece orchestra, with a full string section. Blimey, I'm getting the works this time. I said my hellos to the musicians that I knew and then, with me feeling very humble, Bob Barratt called down for a rehearsal run through, so I quickly made my way to a sound booth to separate me from the orchestra. In those days the singer did not have the luxury of earphones (cans) – it was simple, you just cupped your ear with your hand and sang your heart out. It was just the same when recording broadcasts for the Beeb; nowadays of course, recording is so different and so much easier for the singer. The machinery does all the work. Ha, the mind boggles. Well, back to studio 2 at Abbey Rd. After approximately three hours I had laid down three songs, an extra one in case we needed it. I have to say, the session had gone fantastically and both the principal songs sounded like hits! You know, it's a wonderful feeling to hear your own composition come alive with a full orchestral backing, together with vocal backing singers, just fabulous! Yes, I did forget to mention that I had the Mike Sams Singers on both "She" and "Saving My Tears".

Well, my new single gets released and I go through the usual promotional things, just as I've done before. I also start to get myself a few cabaret bookings, to include a week in a small but nice club in Carlisle, another week at The Gosforth Park Hotel, Newcastle, another week in a nice club in Bournemouth and quite a few one-nighters in some more local clubs. I have to confess, I've not been enjoying this work. For a start it's pretty lonely, having always had the Boys around, and secondly, I do miss the Boys when it comes to backing.

Some of the musicians I'm meeting on the road are not that good and it makes for a tough time when you're out front with a 45-minute spot to do.

It's summer time and both Ann and I decide we would like to go for our first baby – if we are lucky, we could have a springtime birth. Also at about this time, Ann's mother is admitted into hospital in Portsmouth. She had a few problems, including high blood pressure, and would be in for a couple of weeks.

Meanwhile, my latest single is out and selling OK, but nothing to get too excited about yet. The weeks pass and before long we are into autumn time and Ann confirms some good news! She is pregnant! And the baby is due late April 1966. It was not an easy time for Ann, who suffered very bad morning sickness, and it seemed like she was living on Lucozade, which was about all she could keep down. The house at Cheshunt was progressing nicely and should be ready just after Christmas, which will be perfect, giving us time to settle before the baby is due!

However, at the risk of being a complete bore, I have to report the truth; and the truth is my single is not going to make the charts. It has been selling well, but not enough to get into the hit parade. By now I've run out of words to explain my feelings – this really is a good single and I'm bloody gutted!

From out of the blue I get a call from a Mr Peter Bridge, who tells me that he knows all about me and my singing career and would like to meet me with regard to my performing in panto this coming Christmas and New Year. I made an appointment to see him at his home near Chelsea and the meeting took place with him and a very nice lady called Olga Lowe, an actress who had made films, including "Those Magnificent Men in their Flying Machines", remember that one? We talked for a long time about everything I had done in show biz., and then Peter said he would love me to play the part of Wishee-Washee in a production of Aladdin at The Palace Theatre, Westcliff-on-Sea, Essex. He said he would like me also to do a solo ten-minute singing spot. Well, to be honest, I was delighted by the chance to do a bit of acting and have some fun doing it. We agreed financial terms, and he told me that rehearsals would start about the second week of December. I regret, that I'm now going to repeat myself with regard to recording, because I get a call from Bob Barrett, Columbia Records, as I'm sure you are now very well aware, and he wants me to go to his office after working hours with regard to a new recording before Christmas, and even I am beginning to wonder is it all worth the trouble. Bob played me a song, recorded by Frankie Valli and The Four Seasons, a fantastic American group, who have already had big, big hits. Bob suggested we both sit down for an hour, with him on the old jo-anna and we try to compose a similar song. OK, let's do it. We tossed around a few ideas for a title, then Bob found a nice unusual chord change, and in about half an hour we had come up with a song, completely different from anything I had recorded before. Its title was "It Ain't That Easy". We both believed that this being my very last chance with EMI Records, it was well worth trying something new and different; and this was indeed different! We sorted out another number for the B side and Bob said he would call Ivor Raymond again to do a full orchestral backing with singers. Well, I know I'm repeating myself, but I just couldn't believe what he was saying; orchestras don't come cheap and to date my track record for hits is pretty poor. Oh well, who am I to question what they spend? Let's do it! When I arrived at studio 2, Abbey Rd., I was this time expecting to see a big orchestra, but did not expect to see my vocal backing as The Ivy League, a vocal trio made up of some very good mates, Perry Ford, John Carter and Ken Lewis; they themselves had just had a big hit record with "Tossin and Turnin", I'm sure you will recall that one!

Well, the session went well enough, but I found the very high range and falsetto required pushed me to my limits, and to this day I've always felt that I needed a little more studio time and some inspirational production to have made this a real winner. Had it been today, with modern recording techniques, it would have been all very easy and a great result, I'm sure. However, though not completely happy, the record was released as "It Ain't That Easy" and on the B side a song called "And Then". I will now do my best to promote the single, with of course the help of the great EMI Ltd. The record got a mixed reception from the music industry, but more importantly, would the public like it and buy it? It didn't take too long to find out. Within a month of release we all knew it was going to be another Bismarck and take a dive. However, this time, although disappointed, I knew we were taking a chance trying something different and, as my old boss at the nursery, Mr Mason, once said to me, "Sainty, to try and to fail is no disgrace," and I've always remembered those words. Yes indeed, I really have tried very hard and most probably will not get another opportunity. I thank all those people and record companies who, over the past six years, have stood by me and shown faith in me. We all tried very hard.

Now, I think this is the perfect time to tell you about Relevant Information, a term I used in my comments at the end of 1964 regarding my failing records and the emotional turmoil this has put me through at times. I will now tell you the reason for all this. Early in 1960, together with The Nu-Notes, I recorded "Itsy Bitsy Teeny Weeny Yellow Polka Dot Bikini", but for reasons known only to my recording company at that time, namely, Decca, my single didn't get released, so Hit Number One was missed!

Later that same year, I recorded together with The Nu-Notes another great song called "The Girl of my Best Friend". However, because Elvis Presley recorded the song just before my version was to be released, Decca Records decided for whatever reason to pull the plug and my single did not get released. Incidentally, my version was different and a bit faster than the massive hit that Elvis had. Hit Number Two missed!

In 1962, whilst doing my weekly trip to all the music publishers in Denmark Street, Kassner Music Ltd. offered me a demo of an American recording. The song was called "Roses Are Red". I took this to my then recording manager, Walter Ridley at HMV records who said, "Yes, it's OK, I will think about using it with you." Meanwhile, both Bobby Vinton and Ronnie Carroll had big hits with the song. Yes, Hit Number Three missed!

It's now 1964; I'm visiting Ron Lockyer at Southern Music Ltd. in Denmark St. He takes me in to see songwriter Geoff Stevens, who played me a demo of a new song he had just composed. It was called "The Crying Game". I made the comment, "It sounds a bit like a Roy Orbison song," to which Geoff replied, "Yes Russ, but you can arrange it to suit yourself". I said "Geoff, can I take it to my recording manager, Walter Ridley?" and he agreed. Walter liked the song and said, "Russ, we will use this at your next recording session." Meanwhile, unbeknown to me, Dave Berry recorded the song and it became a massive hit. Hit Number Four missed!

Now that you, my reader, know the facts, I feel sure you will appreciate just why I have been on such a roller coaster emotional ride for so many years. Knowing now how four very big hit songs slipped through my fingers, but through no fault of my own. I sincerely hope this recording saga is not overdone in my story, but it being probably the most important thing in any singing career, I felt that I should try to go through and explain each record that I made in detail.

Now having poured my heart out on this subject of hit songs that I missed, I have to say it is a fact that there is possibly more interest in my early records now than at the time they were released. This interest in "The Retro Period", those wonderful heady pioneering Rock 'n' Roll days of the mid fifties through to the early sixties, seems to be worldwide! It's wonderful to know that there is a massive audience out there, who may be collectors or people who simply love to play those early Rock vinyls. Everyone will have an opinion as to why this should be, including me, and I will explain just why I believe those early records are now so special to so many people, both young and old. Speaking from experience, when I first heard those early American Rock 'n' Roll records, I just wanted desperately to be a part of this new pop music phenomenon

– it was nothing to do with making money or celebrity status, it was simply something new, exciting and for the young people of our nation, following those dark days of war with Germany. Those of us who did become involved didn't realise at the time just what we were getting into, since Rock 'n' Roll would change the public perception of popular music forever.

This leads me to our early records, which we recorded on the wave of excitement, enthusiasm and naivety that surrounded the music industry at that time. Clearly, the recording techniques in those early Rock 'n' Roll days were completely different from those of today, and in my opinion this is one of the ingredients that make those early records so special – they have a sound all of their own, and it's great. When recording at that time, we would do a complete performance in the studio, "mistakes and all", unlike today when the whole industry is money motivated and recordings are produced digitally and computer perfect; a singer today doesn't even have to sing in tune, since this can be easily corrected with today's modern technology and equipment. I personally have no axe to grind over this; it's simply progress I guess. Another reason which makes our early records so special is the fact that, in those days, there were only a handful of us British Rock 'n' Roll singers about; for instance, I was just about the only singer in Leyton, my home town, to be actually making records, whereas today just about every home in the nation has a son or daughter who sings or wants to become a "Celebrity". It is no longer "special", as it was for myself and my fellow Rock 'n' Roll pioneers of those early days. Just imagine it, there I was in the year 1960, making my way to Decca Studios in London, to record the songs "Don't Believe Him Donna" and "Your Other Love", a B side and as I walk into the studio, I'm faced with a twenty five-piece orchestra, and the Mike Sams Singers for my backing vocals! There was sheer fright running through my body, a mere Rock 'n' Roll singer with very little experience facing this daunting task, since remember that in those days the singer would be partitioned off into a separate box with windows, and it was difficult to hear the music clearly with no headphones to wear, and we would have to cup one hand around an ear as an aid to hear what we were doing, since all the vocals and instrumental backing were recorded together, unlike today!

Just another ingredient, in my opinion, which makes my early records and those of my fellow musicians and singers more popular now than ever, is that, like any good wine, I'm told that they sound even better as the years pass by.

Yes indeed, our early recordings are very exciting, original and from the heart, and like anything that is "The First", interest and the desire to have and play those early records will surely grow; after all they are British Rock 'n' Roll's history, good enough reason in itself for their growing popularity, and long may it continue.

Now back to normality. Ann's parents have moved out of their pub and taken on a gift shop and restaurant business on Hayling Island, where of course Ann was brought up. Ann is still having bad morning sickness and continues to work in the garage in Lea Bridge Rd. It's December and I start rehearsals for panto at Westcliff-on-Sea, Essex. Rehearsals have gone well and in a few days we will have our opening night. It's 22nd December. I arrive back to our flat in Clapton and Ann has a lovely dinner ready for me. It's about 6.30pm and we get a phone call. Ann takes the call; I see her face drop and a scream of "No, No, No". It was Mary, Ann's sister, phoning to tell us that her mum had died suddenly, whilst writing her Christmas cards. It seems that she had a massive haemorrhage to the brain and had no chance of recovery. As you would expect, we were both in a state of shock. So much so, I can't remember what happened for a day or two. It was very difficult for me as we were now about to do our first night with the panto, Aladdin, and I was struggling with my emotions, but I did get by and the show was a big success on opening night, thank God!

It's panto season 1965/6.
Photos showing the programme for the show.

Two pictures showing Russ in the panto, Aladdin, and playing the part of Wishee Washee.

What a way to end 1965. Like I said much earlier in my story, life is full of surprises – some good and some bad, this was sadly the latter. However, as this was the last year for Russ Sainty to appear at the California Ballroom, I would like to make a final summary of those wonderful times. Firstly, let's check out this year's statistics and I can confirm that even though Russ Sainty only had three (3) bookings, equating to six (6) 45-minute sets, no other performer did more than myself; in fact Zoot Money Big Roll Band did three bookings, like myself. So there we have it, starting in 1960 through to and including 1965, I did more performances for each of those fantastic years than any other artiste, a total of one hundred and sixty-nine (169) bookings, equating to three hundred and thirty-eight (338) 45-minute separate sets. Wowie, just incredible and I'm glowing with pride!

I have to say, I've always wondered just how did Eddy Green get to know about Russ Sainty and The Nu-Notes in the first place. He was a very shrewd business man and he clearly did some homework before making his journey to Romford in Essex just to see us playing in the early winter

above Cast of the panto look on as a cake is presented to the principal dame, Clarkson Rose, on his birthday. Russ can be seen helping to blow out the candles. Definitely not Rock 'n' Roll, but good fun.

right Clarkson Rose gives Russ his autograph. February 1966.

months of 1960. Opening the 'Cali' was indeed a massive venture and for us to be chosen as the Rock 'n' Roll group to perform at the opening night of such a big investment was firstly, as it turned out, a wonderful piece of judgement by Mr Green and secondly, a turning point for Russ Sainty and The Nu-Notes. Let us not lose sight of the fact that we were never booked as a resident band. Our bookings were all one offs and block bookings, and to think that for six years we retained our popularity, playing alongside the biggest names in the popular music business of the day, including America's best. This was indeed special and I once again reiterate how proud I am to be a massive part of the California Ballroom history. I had a wonderful fan base in the area, for which I will always be grateful and certainly never ever forget and I had a super relationship with the Green family. They always made me feel welcome and at home and, to be honest, I always felt like part of the family.

The California Ballroom, Dunstable, became, I believe, the single most important venue of its kind in the whole of the British Isles. Just about anyone who was anyone in the pop world played at this unique place. It was, of course, equally very special for the paying customers, as I have mentioned before, it had that Home from Home feel. It was a safe, happy, fun environment, a place where lasting friendships were made, a place where couples met for the first time and later married, and a place where people could see the stars of the day performing at touching distance. Very sadly, Eddy Green passed away following a long illness on 21st November 1964, leaving the running to his family. Following my last show at the 'Cali' on 24th April 1965, with Johnny Kidd and The Pirates, I had no more contact with the place, but do know that it eventually changed to be named Soul City and finally closed its doors for good in summer 1979.

In 1983 I was doing a broadcast on local Chiltern Radio and decided to go and see whether or not the 'Cali' was still standing. But not surprisingly, having got to the spot where she once stood, I found myself in a small housing estate. I decided to sit slap bang in the middle of this estate and eat my sandwiches and drink a coffee from my flask. Oh boy! I have to admit to a tear or two, it was indeed a very sad moment for me. In my mind's eye, I could see the old place and hear the music blasting out, and yes, I could see myself singing to a massive audience with the front three rows all crowded around the stage, as they always did – it all seemed so real. But then of course, it once was!

Now finally, it would be remiss of me not to point out – after having written about my personal memories of the 'Cali' with every endeavour to get dates, facts and figures correct – that the California Ballroom still lives on to this very day, nearly 30 years after it closed its doors. There is a book called *The*

'Cali' Album by Diane Ilka, and there are mentions of the 'Cali' in the book, A Hatful of Music by Stuart Goodyear of the Ray Miller Orchestra, and now of course, my own book. Furthermore, there is a wonderful web site devoted to all aspects of the 'Cali', www.california-ballroom.info, webmaster Jaybee. In addition, www.cali-r.com promotes reunion events, organised by former 'Cali' DJ Sid Hudson.

Just one more thing, but I will leave it until a little later in my story. I have a big surprise for you relating to the 'Cali', so please stick with me, it's not to be missed.

* * * * * * * * * * * * *

However, I thought this would be the perfect time to give you a little bit of inside information on some of the happenings to Russ Sainty and The Nu-Notes at the 'Cali'. Let's call this... CALI TIT-BITS

Did you know that soon after we opened the 'Cali' in March 1960, our drummer, Bernie Martin, decided he would try using two bass drums! So on a Saturday night in April, whilst playing on the small stage, he did just that! This probably went unnoticed by most of the audience, but it was in fact a bit special for a very young drummer in a pop group to attempt this, so much so that Bernie always believed that he was probably the first pop group drummer to attempt playing with this extended drum kit. Bernie was of course a very talented young drummer, with excellent technique.

*

Did you know that Russ Sainty and The Nu-Notes were possibly the first British pop Rock 'n' Roll group to use an echo box? This fact was confirmed by Jennings Musical Instruments, of Charing Cross Road, London, who were the sellers of this equipment. This all happened late 1958 when we were performing at many of the American military bases, where the Yanks could not believe just where the fantastic big sound was coming from. Of course, by the time we were performing at the 'Cali' early 1960, The Nu-Notes and in particular Rhet Stoller had perfected the use of this piece of equipment, and I believe that this was a big factor in our success in those early days; the Cali audience would just marvel at the sound we produced. This, together with Bernie Martin's playing two bass drums, was another factor which helped keep us ahead of any competition. Of course other groups would see what we were doing and they too would try to catch up, to name just two in question, Brian Poole and The Tremeloes and of course a local group called The Barron Knights. They would watch us perform and then ask questions about our equipment etc. etc. and guess what, they, like a few others, made it right to the top with hit records coming out of their ears! Good luck to you guys, glad we helped along the way.

*

Did you know that our bass player, "Mad" Mel Miller, played the big old fashioned double bass when we first performed at the 'Cali' in 1960. It wasn't until early 1961 that he bought a brand new Fender electric bass, and at the same time both Rhet Stoller and Roy Toft, our two guitarists, bought Fender electric guitars. These early original Fender instruments are now worth a fortune.

*

Did you know that in 1961 at the 'Cali' down on the small stage, I sang the hit song for Bobby Vee called "More Than I Can Say". OK, so what, I can hear you saying. Well, this time it was different, let me explain just why. I did in fact sing to the backing of The Nu-Notes as normal, but as an added extra, Rhet Stoller had recorded a backing track for the song using guitars and string sounds, which he did with a small keyboard instrument called a clavichord that he had converted in order to get these violin string sounds. This was, of course, the predecessor to the modern synthesizers and keyboards. He also added what we now understand as a "click", which gave him the tempo when playing the track back through a set of "cans" (earphones). Now, what this did for us was to double our sound with the added extra of beautiful violins, and believe me, the audience were amazed and in awe of this fantastic sound coming from Russ Sainty and The Nu-Notes, and, apart from those at the front of the stage, who could perhaps see the Vortexion Recording Machine being operated by Rhet, nobody else knew what was happening, and must have been looking for a string quartet playing along with us! Again, this was an attempt to keep ahead of the game; we never had a moment to sit back on our laurels as the saying goes. And this was another first. It just didn't happen in 1961, it was simply an idea by Rhet Stoller, and boy did it work! These days, of course, it's commonplace to use what is now known as a Click Track. The Steno Vortexion Recorder, which Rhet used, is in fact the same machine he used on several of his one man albums a year or two later, where he recorded every instrument himself. This is called multi tracking and does require a second machine, at least in those days it did. This same machine may well have been used by Rhet when recording his own composition, now a world wide hit, "Match of the Day", football's very own anthem. After all this, he gave the recorder to me, in order to pay off some cash he owed me. And yes, I do still have that very same recording machine, a little dusty, but in good working order!

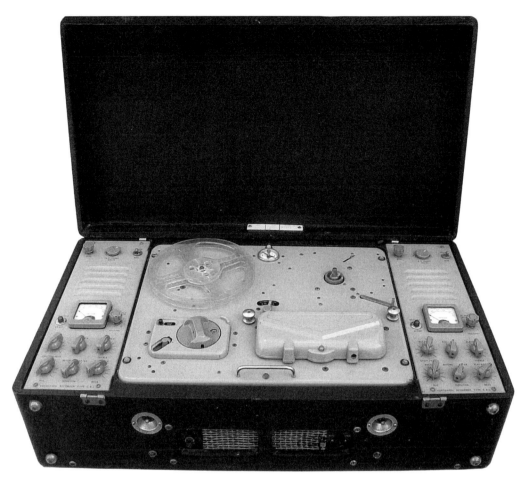

A photograph taken in 2008, showing the Sterio Vortexion tape recording machine as used by Rhet Stoller for so many of his works, including albums, theme tunes for TV advertising, most of the early rehearsals by Russ Sainty and The Nu-Notes and many demos of new songs composed by us all. This machine was also used at the 'Cali' in year 1961 when I sang to both a backing track and the Boys were playing live. It's also quite possible that this machine was one of several used when Rhet composed and recorded the football theme tune Match Of The Day.

*

It's early 1961, and we have what has become a regular Saturday night booking at the California Ballroom. I decide, rather than drive over to Stamford Hill North London, to the Stoller household, where myself and The Nu-Notes meet, then load all our equipment before setting off for the gig in Mr Stoller's Bedford mini bus, that I will make my own way to Dunstable with my girlfriend Ann Graham, using my little Ford Thames van. We set off from my home in Leyton, making our way to the Ml motorway, which in those days was very quiet and a real joy to drive on. After about 50 minutes, I turn off onto the old A5 road, and by now I'm only a few miles from the

'Cali', when suddenly steam comes billowing from the front of my vehicle. "What the hell's happening?" I yelled out, and immediately pulled over to the verge and stopped the engine. Ann and I looked at each other and just laughed, before I jumped out and looked under the bonnet in the hope that I could find the problem. "Oh sh—t," I shouted to Ann, "the bloody fan belt is in shreds and we have over heated." I walked back and jumped into the driving seat, scratching my head and wondering what to do next, and then Ann said to me, "We have only got a few miles to go, what about using one of my stockings tied around to replace the fan belt?" I said, "Ann, I've heard of people doing this before, so let's give it a go." Well, Ann having now removed both stockings, I make my way back to the engine and set about trying to tie one of them in place, and would you "adam and eve it", having now got myself back into the driving seat, with grease everywhere, I started the engine and it went like clockwork. We set off straightaway and in no time at all I was turning left on green at the traffic lights in Dunstable. I continue towards the downs and then a left turn into the 'Cali' car park. Ahh! made it, thank God for that. I rushed into the 'Cali' to find the Boys, who must have wondered where the hell I was, and they fell about laughing. Evidently I had black grease all over my face, which they all thought was extremely funny.

*

Did you know that on the 13th October 1962, following our first 45-minute set on the big stage at the 'Cali', Russ Sainty and The Nu-Notes were given a massive surprise. No, can't remember? OK, let me tell you what this was all about. A little earlier in the year, news correspondent to the Daily Mirror, Patrick Doncaster, gave us a wonderful double page write up, in which he mentioned our new record "Keep Your Love Locked", but the main content of his story was about Russ Sainty and The Nu-Notes becoming a Limited Company. This was indeed headline news at the time, since it was generally believed that we were the very first "Pop-Rock 'n' Roll Group" to actually do such a thing, we were known as R.M.B.MUSIC LTD., the R being taken from Russ and Roy, the M from Mel Miller, and the B from Barry Stoller and Bernie Martin.

How does this all tie in with a surprise at the 'Cali'? Well, I think it would be fair to say that Eddy Green was not one to miss out on an opportunity, and he took the bull by the horns, in this case thinking publicity, publicity, publicity! As we were about to walk off stage, he jumped up and grabbed the microphone, asking us to wait a few minutes, after which he addressed the audience, telling them that following the wonderful recent article in The Daily

Mirror about Russ Sainty and The Nu-Notes becoming a Limited Company, he had a little surprise for us. With that, he asked Mrs Green to unveil a brand new office desk and present this to me as leader of the group and secretary of our new company. This was indeed a wonderful gesture by "The Boss and his wife" and good publicity all round, I would say; the audience certainly loved all the "bally-hoo".

*

Do you remember The Spotnicks? No, they're not from outer space, they were in fact a top Swedish Group who had a few hits. One of them being an instrumental called "Orange Blossom Special", a real exciting and pulsating up tempo number. When speaking to Roger Dean, Nu-Notes lead guitarist, just recently, we discussed the Saturday night when we played with them at the 'Cali'; both of us recall what happened that night, but neither of us can recall the date. We can only work out that it would have been late 1962, the year The Spotnicks had that particular hit, or possibly 1963. OK Russ, what did happen on whatever date it might have been? I hear you saying. Alright, I'm now going to explain. I remember it well, myself and The Nu-Notes standing over by the dressing room (kitchen) door listening to the group, and we all made comments about what we thought of them, which I have to tell you was pretty average. However, things were about to become very embarrassing. One of the group introduced their big hit number "Orange Blossom Special" and away they went, with ourselves and a very big audience all watching and listening on. Well, I have to tell you the truth, it was a joke. The lead guitarist was not able to actually play the number properly, it was all over the place, and as I have already mentioned, a little embarrassing all round.

This being the last number of their performance meant that we followed them on stage to do the last session of the evening. After doing a few numbers ourselves, Roger Dean shouted to the rest of us, "What about we do our version of "Orange Blossom Special"?" A few of the audience heard this and started to shout, "Yeh, do it Rog, come on show them how to play the number." Then, before I could say hold on a minute, The Nu-Notes were into it and there was no stopping them. Well, I have to say, Roger, our lead guitarist, did a fantastic job, and as the number came to an end the audience went mad, whistling and shouting for more, which was all very nice at the time, but on reflection, at the end of the evening, we all felt it was the wrong thing to have done, even though the 'Cali' audience loved us for doing it. Oh well, happy days!

*

FAREWELL TO THE 'CALI' AND THE NO. 1 DREAM

The date is 9th August 1963, it's our second appearance with The Rolling Stones at the 'Cali', and you may recall in my earlier text, I made the comment that unlike the first time we appeared together, just two weeks previous on 27th July, this particular evening was not quite so memorable. Well, having had a long chat to our bass player Mel Miller, when researching this particular piece, he reminded me that there was a "Cali Happening" on that particular evening, something that I can't believe. Now it's all flooding back into my mind, so I will explain all. We were down to appear on the small stage that evening and would open up proceedings doing the first set, so decided to go into our prop box and sort out a nice wig for each of us to wear, as a bit of a "send up", knowing The Stones would be following us. Well, as you will see in the photo taken that night, it really was quite funny, and as usual our Cali audience were all behind us and went along with the joke. At the end of our set, we get a big round of applause and make our way over to the dressing room (kitchen) and as we push the door open to make our way inside, The Stones were just about to make their way out and onto the big stage. We passed each other, touching shoulders as we did so, with Mick Jagger bringing up the rear; then, just as he passed Mel Miller of The Nu-Notes, Mick made the comment to him, "Are you taking the piss mate?" to which Mel replied, "No just the micky!" to which we all fell about giggling our heads off. Of course, as we all know, they later had the last laugh, by achieving those heady heights of Rock 'n' Roll fame, fortune and longevity, not forgetting Mick's knighthood. Which all goes to show, that he who laughs last, sometimes laughs longest. Keep Rockin'!

*

Mad Mel Miller, The Nu-Notes bass player of course, but please don't think for one minute that Mel was a nutter; he was in fact anything but. He somehow adopted the tag of "Mad Mel" because of his constant larking about. He was always the joker of the group, who would do strange things, like walking into a newsagent's shop and asking in a very serious voice for the Gangster Gazette or the Prisoners Weekly, and, if they didn't have it, would they please order it for him? I recall on many occasions, when sitting down in a restaurant, he would tell the waitress that he wanted a bunch of fresh raw carrots for his six foot rabbit "Harvey", and he would be very persistent about it, driving the waitress crazy at times. None of us knew quite what he was about to do or say next. I also recall Mel being carried around the 'Cali' ballroom by one of the bouncers, a lovely man called Fred, who was at the 'Cali' for years. It's quite possible that you, my dear reader, may well remember the night Mel was leaping about on

This photo shows Russ and the Boys performing in wigs as a bit of a send up when appearing with the Rolling Stones for the second time at the 'Cali' in 1963.

the 'Cali''s small stage like a complete lunatic when suddenly, without any warning, he fell through the stage floor! Ouch! Of course, the audience thought it was all part of our act, but in fact it was far from it. Mel cut his leg badly, and still has the scar to this day. A bit too late to put in a claim Mel? On another occasion at the 'Cali', Mel told me that he had a great number to do, and asked me if he could have the microphone. Strangely, he started to read out the football results, starting very slowly and in a very distinguished voice, but gradually he started to speed up until eventually he was screaming out the results at the top of his voice, with his eyes popping out of his head, and arms waving like windmills. So strange, but the audience loved it, and this typified Mel Miller at his best; crazy days and just another "Cali Happening". P.S. Mel Miller was also a great bass player!

*

The Bachelors, a group of three Irishmen who had some massive hit records during the sixties, like "Charmaine", "I Believe", " Diane" and others. They appeared at the 'Cali' on 27th April 1963, along with ourselves, who would both perform on the big stage, together with Neil Christian and The Crusaders, who performed on the small stage at the far end of the ballroom. Following Neil Christian's first set, we then took over and did our first set. On completing this, we walked back to the dressing room, passing The Bachelors, who were making their way to the big stage. I then stopped and watched, thinking to myself, "Where is their vocal equipment?" They then started fiddling with our equipment and placing our microphones around to suit them. Meanwhile of course, I had switched everything off, as I always did when leaving the stage. By now, the audience were getting a bit twitchy as every minute's silence seemed like an hour. I decided to walk over and speak to them, asking "What's going on, that's our equipment you are messing around with?" to which they replied, "Yes perhaps it is, but we need it switched on." Well I have to tell you, by now I was furious and told them in no uncertain words, "You are not using our stuff, why did you not bring your own equipment or at least have the decency to ask me before you went on stage?" Here was a very successful group, making lots of big money, and simply turning up expecting to use other people's equipment, and in our case we were still paying for it on hire purchase! They then decided they would use the Cali's own house system, which to be honest was not very good, but that was their problem, not ours. We did of course let other performers use our equipment, provided they asked us in good time, but on this occasion the sheer arrogance shown by The Bachelors was just too much to take.

*

The 'Cali' Dressing Room: you will have gathered by now that in truth there wasn't one. Well, let me put it this way, during the six years 1960 to 1965 inclusive that I performed there, we always used the 'Cali' kitchens as our dressing room, so if there was a real one tucked away somewhere, Russ Sainty and The Nu-Notes never ever found it! It wasn't ideal, but I can confirm that during those cold winter nights, as soon as we arrived to take in our stage clothes, we would light up just about all of the gas rings in order to get the place warmed up, so in that respect I guess we had to be thankful. Of course, the big name acts always used to get changed in the Greens' bungalow. Well, couldn't expect them to change in the 'Cali' kitchens, they might well have got some grease on their clothes. Happy Days, we had no complaints, simply an observation.

*

How did our Cali days come to an end? A question I've been asked many times over the years, and the answer is quite easy, let me explain again. Early in the New Year of 1965, the Boys and I discussed our situation and made the decision that we would break up and as I've already documented, I told The Nu-Notes that we would do this following our last booking at the 'Cali', April 24th 1965. Of course, some weeks previous, I had informed Mrs Green what was going to happen, and that we would not be able to accept any bookings following that date. I do recall her disappointment and a tinge of sadness to learn about the break up. After all, we were like family, and had been a massive part of this unstoppable phenomenon in the pop Rock 'n' Roll business, a venue called the California Ballroom, Dunstable, Bedfordshire. But like all good things, it did finally come to an end.

Russ in cabaret during the 1970s.

Chapter Twelve

SOLO AFTER THE 'CALI' YEARS

OK time to take stock of my situation, with my backing group The Nu-Notes now retired to greener pastures (or maybe not so green?). I'm now a solo performer, I've already had lots of cabaret bookings, and acted as" Wishee-Washie" in Aladdin for a six-week run. I'm also a married man; oh, my wife Ann is pregnant (planned of course), and my days at the California Ballroom are over. A good time perhaps to consider, have I made any money out of this Rock 'n' Roll malarkey during the past eight years? After all, to date, I've had ten singles 45rpm records on the market, not including any instrumentals, and one album of Beatles songs. Of my singles, I've composed eight of the songs myself. I also composed "Fury" which was a Nu-Notes instrumental release, together with four other songs I composed and have had released on 45rpm singles for other singers. So with all those royalties coming in for records released and for my own published songs, I should be pretty rich. Ha ha, don't hold your breath, let me tell you what really happened. In truth, I can't recall receiving a single penny for any of the singles I recorded, even though I had real contracts with the like of Decca and EMI Records. Furthermore, I have never received more than around £50 in total for all my published songs. This may surprise you, my dear reader, but believe me, this is the truth. The fact is, having spoken to dozens of my fellow singers and musicians from this early period of Rock 'n' Roll, it appears that none of us got what we should have got by way of royalties; most of us were conned out of what was rightfully ours. However, I have to also admit that I, for one, was singing Rock 'n' Roll because I loved doing it, and it was only in later years that the reality of the situation dawned on me, and in this respect, I know, I'm speaking for most of my fellow singer/musicians of that early era. But for all the losses, we all made a decent living, of course some better than others.

Well, I can tell you that, due to family circumstances and after much

left Summer 1966, Russ and Ann at our fruit stall situated on our restaurant forecourt.
right The restaurant on Hayling Island which Ann and I took over in spring of 1966, following the passing away of Ann's Mother.

consideration, I decided to move down to Hayling Island on the south coast, and join my father-in-law in the catering business, though this was never ever going to stop me from singing; in fact, I still had BBC broadcasts booked for many months ahead.

In 1968, I was approached by Vick Flick, the guitarist for The John Barry Seven, who came down to our house at Hayling Island, where we planned my next single 45rpm recording. But first I would go to a well known recording studio in London and "demo" about half a dozen songs that he and a drummer called Duggie Wright had composed. From these "demos", two songs were chosen for my single, an A and a B side, called "We're Falling in Love" and "I Can Give You a Love", which were then recorded with full orchestra, and the single was released under the RIM Records label, a branch of Rediffusion Ltd. (Please see Discography for all record details). How did the record sell, you may ask. Err. Answer, just like all the others! Oh well, life goes on, and for the next ten years I perform cabaret at most of those infamous Northern Working Men's Clubs of the day (which I hated doing), as well as, shall we say, some proper night clubs. These included the Bailey Clubs, one of which was at Watford, not a million miles from Dunstable and the 'Cali'. I also did several song festivals during this period, both in Gibraltar and Southern Ireland, namely The Castle Bar and Cavan Song Festivals, on the west coast of Ireland, which were great fun and gave me some welcome TV exposure.

LYN PARKER

CLIVE PETERSON

RUSS SAINTY

above and left The Gibraltar Song Festival programme, 1971.

below Russ in action singing one of two numbers in the final of The Gibraltar Festival.

News Page for Women

Russ set for a comeback

Remember the name, Russ Sainty? Team it with The Nu-Notes and perhaps that will jar your memory a little harder. That's it . . . gently swinging pop star of the early 60's.

So whatever happened to HIM, you may ask. And why mention his name now, nearly a decade after his abrupt departure from the pop scene?

Explanation: Russ Sainty, now 34 years old, resident of Hayling Island, father of two children, owner of a boutique and a take-away hot snacks shop, is going back into show business.

Reason: His appetite for the entertainment world has been revived by a successful taster performance at the world Gibraltar Song Festival. He was invited by a friend to sing two songs put on demonstration records some years ago — and they were placed fourth and fifth.

"I've got the confidence now to try to break back into the business. Everyone said I did well at the Festival and it has been just the booster I needed." he says, almost singing out his enthusiasm to tackle the new twist his life has taken.

Fairly well

It wasn't a conscious decision on his part to opt out of pop and into trading those six years ago come January. He and his wife had just moved to Hayling to open a children's boutique, and he was booked to play Wishy-Washy in an Aladdin pantomime in which Clarkson Rose was the Dame.

The pop business up to that point, had treated him and his group fairly well. During the seven years they had been in it, they had had a reasonable slice of the TV-radio-concert tour cake — but never a hit record. It concerned Russ that they had never found the right song and the right sound to take them into the hit parade. "But on all other counts," he recalled, "we had no complaints."

The Hayling boutique enterprise chiefly involved his wife Ann, and her parents who were to help her run it and the restaurant next door. Everything seemed to be working out until

"just the day before the panto was due to open, Ann's mother died. It was a pretty awful time. I did the panto and then went to Hayling to help out. Ann's father decided later on that he didn't want to stay, so I remained at Hayling to help Ann and kind of drifted out of show business. Everything just folded up — force of circumstances really."

And everything, as far as show business is concerned, has stayed that way for the past six years. In that time, the Saintys have expanded their trading interests to incorporate a take-away snacks shop in Portsmouth (there is a second one

artist — with the right kind of song.

"To get up on the stage in Gibraltar and sing — the first time in public for six years — was a marvellous experience. I thought it would be difficult for me, so did Ann, but when the time came I wasn't that nervous, the style was still there and I slotted back into it.

"I'm more mature now, rather more level-headed and confident. I've got my confidence back. I'm really out to make it this time.

Might he accept a name change if it was thought necessary? "Bury the old name and dinck proved it, was a good move in his case."

Sainty is a Londoner, an East Ender in fact. He was an apprentice jockey in his teens — "But I got too tall and heavy" — and then he took an apprenticeship in horticulture, interrupted for two years by right.

"I would really have liked to continue working with animals. When I was a kid, we didn't

have much of a back garden but I used to keep rabbits and turkeys and chickens, and go down Petticoat Lane on a Sunday to flog them.

Pub

"I got my first taste for singing when I stood up in a pub and did a couple of songs. Eventually, I didn't have to bother with the horticulture any more, though I enjoyed it. I turned to show business full-time.

His wife, he says, is more than pleased that he has decided to try to make a comeback. "She's been telling me to do this for ages, and at last I've reached a decision. I don't expect it to be easy but Ann is sure I shall get back into the business.

"Why's that saying?" He paused for a moment. "Oh yes — you know, something about there being a determined woman behind every successful man. Ann is determined all

— Jane Hunt

Russ Sainty, at home at Hayling Island with son Darren, aged three. He is hopeful about making a comeback into show business. 55351-1

Solo

"I'm lucky in one thing — I still have contacts in the business, and I'm going to cultivate them," he says candidly. "I've got in mind the song I'd like to record, an Ed Welch number, and as soon as I can get confirmation of that, then things will really start moving.

The groups tend to dominate, but people like Humperdinck, Tom Jones, Andy Williams, and Cliff Richard are proving that there is still room for the solo

below A long shot of Russ at The Gibraltar Festival, where the numbers he sang finished 3rd and 4th, oh well, not bad I guess.

In 1976, following a "showcase" that I did up in Lancashire, I was offered a three month booking on The QE2, or three months in South Africa. I chose the latter. I first went to Durban and had a wonderful time in a club beneath The Beach Hotel on the sea front, where I did thirteen shows a week for six weeks, after which I went to Cape Town and did like-wise, in a club beneath The Century Hotel, at Sea Point, beneath the famous "lions back" mountain. After a six-week run, I returned to Durban for a months booking at The Smugglers Inn. On my return home to Hayling Island, following a short break, I decided to go back to my roots in horticulture, and start up a new business called "Greenacres Landscapes and Garden Maintenance", which went really well, and in no time at all, after taking on a big contract to maintain all Warner Holiday sites on Hayling Island, I had around a dozen staff, which gave me the time to continue with my career in show business.

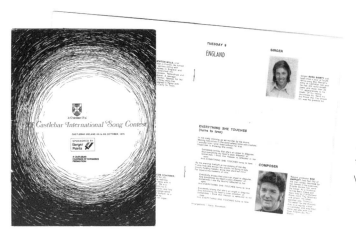

A programme of the Castle Bar International Song Contest, where I finished 3rd in the final with a song called "Let Your Fingers Do The Walking", 1976.

Springtime 1978, back to Southern Ireland for the Cavan International Song Contest: can't keep a good man down, though my song, composed again by Bob Barratt, called "Conchita" didn't get in the top four, shame!

Old friend from those EMI recording days and song composer, Bob Barratt with Russ at the Cavan Festival. Spring 1978.

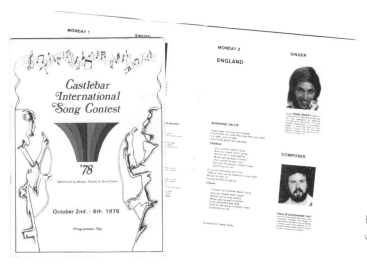

Yes, I'm back to Ireland for yet another song contest, but this time I will be singing for a different composer, Phillip Goodhand-Tait and the song was "Sunshine on Ice"; a finalist but we didn't win.

It's year 1977, Russ and The Nu-Notes meet up for a first time re-union since the split back in 1965, enjoying a night at London's Playboy club. L to R are Bernie Martin, Roy Toft, Russ Sainty, Mel Miller and Rhet Stoller. Roger Dean was working abroad.

Also at this time, since my return from South Africa, I started building a new home, on land I had previously purchased. This meant selling up the house we were living in and moving into a caravan that was parked on site at Queensway, North Hayling Island. This was for me a massive task since I did a lot of the jobs myself; running the project, personally making all the balastrades to complete building the front wall and then to complete the job, landscaping a very large plot into a beautiful garden.

It's springtime 1977, the house that Russ built. No, not all of it, but I did help, and also designed it (clever dick). Photo shows roof going on.

Oh dear, not a pretty sight! Russ looking rather knackered, sitting beside the temporary caravan home, this ain't rock 'n' roll.

It's 1979, the house is finished and I've even built a nice balustrade wall.

Later 1979, I have completed landscaping the garden and also built a nice little bar on the patio, most important!

My cabaret work continued, with amongst other bookings all The Warner Holiday sites in the south, and others including Butlins and Pontins. In 1981, following an audition in The Connaught Rooms in Tottenham Court Road London, I was offered a nine months contract to perform cabaret on board a ship called Amerikanis, sailing out of Miami, Florida to The Bahamas every week. This was great fun, but I did miss the family, and after about six months,

It's late December 1981, Russ joins the cruise liner Amerikanis, based in Miami, Florida.
above Amerikanis docks in The Bahamas, early 1982.
below right On board Amerikanis during March 1982, Russ is seen with Matt Monro, and cruise director, Derek Dean.

above Russ in cabaret at a Warner Holiday Centre on the Isle of Wight, note the audience, not really Rock 'n' Roll, but it's work!

below Yes this is me, dressed for cabaret, well it is the '70s glam rock and all that jazz!

springtime 1982, I returned home, having negotiated by telephone to take over as entertainments manager for Warner Holidays, Sinah Warren, just a few minutes down the road from our house on Hayling Island. Whilst still doing this job, I recorded a new single, called "The 50s Hits, Right Here on 45", a compilation of many late fifties hit songs. I believe that this was probably my most commercial record to date, and one I had produced and put out on my own independent label, "Russ Records". However, though I sold thousands of copies at Sinah Warren after each show and the record was a regular play on the Beeb, I had failed to get a good distributor, meaning the shops were unable to obtain the record, so guess what, it didn't make the charts, through on this occasion a failing I was partly responsible for.

Publicity shot of Russ for new single, "The 50s Hits Right Here on 45", 1983.

Following my few years at Sinah Warren, I decided to take cabaret work which was within about 150 miles radius of my home; which was not at all difficult, with all the many holiday centres on the south coast, this would mean I had some input into the running and working of my ground and maintenance business. Even better, having worked cabaret for them during the 1970s, and then working as Entertainments Manager for several years during the early 1980s at Warners Premier Centre, namely Sinah Warren, I've now been booked to do cabaret for the entire Warner Holiday Circuit, which included all centres on the Isle of Wight. Now, I have to tell you that on many occasions, having done a cabaret spot on say a Monday night, I would have to be at that same centre, the next morning, to organise my staff who might be grass cutting or weeding flower beds, and without fail somebody would recognise me from the previous night, saying, "Oh hello, you look just like the chap who did cabaret last night, you were great." Well, it was flattering, but I would always deny that it was me, and tell the people that it was my brother. Yes, I know it was a white lie, but I thought it was the best thing to do and it did not spoil the perception of the person that they had enjoyed that previous evening!

Summer 1982, photo showing my son Darren, my wife Ann and myself in the jeep. Business with Greenacres continues despite all my show biz commitments.

A view of Warner's premier holiday centre in the 80s, Sinah Warren, on Hayling Island. My place of work as both Entertainments Manager and as a Cabaret Act from the 1970s through to 2008 and I'm not done yet.

My trips to the Isle of Wight, twice a week, could also be quite a laugh with so many holiday resorts on the island; there would sometimes be a half dozen of us cabaret acts meeting up on the ferry from Portsmouth, and then we would all try to meet up again at the end of the evening, rushing to the ferry terminal from all over the island, trying to catch the last ferry back to mainland Portsmouth. As you can guess, so many times one or two of us would not make it, and so would have to catch an early morning ferry, oh dear, not good!

Some of my Greenacres team neatly lined up for a brochure photograph.
L to R, my son Darren, Paul Roberts, Darren Murray and Malcolm Wheeler 1982.

left and below Russ performing cabaret at a club on the south coast 1983.

opposite Russ Sainty with two of his team dancers, Debbie and Tammy. The place, yes you guessed, it's Sinah Warren 1983.

above Russ doing a number with Duke D'mond and The Barron Knights, when they visited Warner's Sinah Warren 1984, just like the 'Cali' days all over again!

below Russ and guitar legend Bert Weedon meet up again in 1984.

Russ and Ann Sainty take over the running of another Warner Holiday Centre, namely Southlea on Hayling Island 1985.

above It's Hawaiian night at Warner's Southlea Centre, can't you just tell?

below Russ with wife Ann and team of entertainers, hi de hi! No, not really, but we did have great fun doing four shows a week and running a full programme.

The News
Central South

DAY, DECEMBER 29, 1986 ● The News Centre, Portsmouth 664488 Phonads 664422) ● Petersfield 62424 (Phonads 56331) No. 34,101 (Est. 1877) 16p

Clowns give children something to smile at

CLOWNS TOOK seasonal cheer to the children's ward at Queen Alexandra Hospital, Cosham, yesterday.

Big-hearted holidaymakers at Warner's Sinah Warren Hotel at Hayling Island dipped into their pockets to raise £185 for the ward - and the hotel's entertainments staff, dressed as clowns, went along to deliver it and to cheer up children

who had to spend Christmas in hospital.

Entertainer Al Page even brought along his balloons and made animal models for the children.

And there was a special surprise for Sinah's sports complex manageress, Mary Jones, who was rushed to the hospital for an emergency operation after she collapsed on Christmas Eve.

The clowns - including her sister,

Mrs. Ann Sainty, and brother-in-law Russ, Sinah's entertainments managers - paid her a special visit and presented the staff on her ward with a hamper from Warner's.

Said Mrs. Sainty: "We decided to make the collection and visit after Mary was taken ill.

"We're all absolutely exhausted after saying goodbye to the 650 guests we had for Christmas - and waiting for the arrival of another 650 for New Year!"

● Sinah Warren entertainments managers Russ and Ann Sainty hand over the cheque to Sister Ruby Hawkes, with a little help from Jolene Holt (seven) and Lymara Anderson (two), and watched by Samantha Williams (back left) and Michelle Sainty (back right) at Queen Alexandra Hospital children's ward. — Photo sales no. 0042-1

below A Christmas special back at Warners Sinah Warren. Russ is back as entertainments manager for a few weeks, seen here running a competition with the girls, 1986.

opposite Another competition, this time with the boys, lunch time already?

left Russ and wife Ann dressed to rob the rich. Robin Hood and Maid Marion take to the floor at Sinah Warren, dig the tights.

above Yes, it's party time again at Warners Sinah Centre, not a pretty sight, Halloween I guess?

left Oh dear, it's Scottish weekend at Warner Holidays, Russ and Ann get into the spirit of the occasion. Note the wellies, definitely not Rock 'n' Roll.

opposite Russ back in the old routine, at a guess he must be singing that old chestnut, "Yankee Doodle Dandy", 1986.

By the late 1980s and early 1990s I was now working with some old mates, namely The Dallas Boys, Craig Douglas, The Vernons Girls and sometimes The Kaye Sisters. We were all working together on a show called "The Oh Boy Show". Myself compering the show and doing my own 20-minute spot. This was a super show, and we had a real ball doing it all over the country. During 1991, The Dallas Boys and myself recorded an album called, "A Pot of Pure Gold" and we sold thousands of copies at the gigs.

By the year 1993, the lead singer of The Dallas Boys, Bob Wragg, decided to retire to his cottage on The Isle of Man, and it was at this time I was asked to step in and take his place, so becoming a member of this wonderful cabaret act. It took me two weeks solid hard work to learn all the songs and the complicated stage moves. After working with the boys for several weeks, I became a complete part of the act. On the downside, I now found myself travelling hundreds of miles every week, it seemed that almost all the shows we did were up North or in deepest Wales. For instance, one year we were booked every Sunday night for The Butlins Hotel in Blackpool and this for me, living in the south, was a six-hundred-mile round trip just for a one-nighter and that was for 26 continuous weeks. Oh, the glamour of being a Rock 'n' Roll singer!

The Dallas Boys

above Early 1990s, Russ
Sainty becomes a Dallas
Boy. L to R, Russ Sainty,
Nicky Clark, Brian Adams,
Paul Greaves and in front
is Richard Fairbrother.

right A promotional
"give-away" postcard
picture for the album
release, A Pot of Pure
Gold. 1991/2.

Russ on stage at Eastbourne, during one of the "Oh Boy" Rock 'n' Roll shows.

above The Dallas Boys in action, 1993.

below Show a leg! The Dallas Boys in cabaret perform their dance routine.

I have to say that after a few years the travelling was getting me down and both my wife Ann and I decided a change of direction was due. I went to see a very good friend, Chris Summerfield, who not only is a wonderful musician but also had a very well equipped recording studio. I had decided to get Chris to record for me a complete, one-hour cabaret act. The songs I had chosen for this were really going to take me back to my roots, "Rock 'n' Roll". Yes, some nice ballads as well, in fact a real mix of material that I loved.

Well, with my backing tracks completed to a very high standard and having purchased the very best sound deck and equipment, I was all set to go out as a solo act, completely self contained. It was at this stage I told The Dallas Boys I would soon be taking bookings as a solo act once more, but I was happy to do both until the boys found a replacement for me. Well, by the end of the year 1995, I had to make the break from the boys, because I was now getting plenty of bookings coming in for Russ Sainty, and on 31st December did my last show as a Dallas Boy. Now, with Ann working my sound equipment, we were busy every week and most importantly it was all local bookings. In fact most weekends for the next six years or so, I would be booked for cabaret in Bournemouth, performing for Masonic functions at just about all the main hotels in the area.

During the springtime of 1996, I get a phone call from a good friend who runs the entertainment at Butlins, and he asked me this question, "Russ, how would you like to have your own one-hour show for a 27-week season at Butlins, Bognor Regis?" After a deep breath, I managed to pick myself up off the floor and replied, "Is this a joke, or what?" He said, "No, I want you to put together a non stop, one-hour Rock 'n' Roll Spectacular. You will have eight dancers – four boys and four girls – and be accompanied by a big ten-piece band. The whole show will be choreographed and full costumes provided."

Well, I was so excited and immediately started to put the show together, and very soon I started rehearsals with all my dancers and our choreographer. What makes this so very very special for me is the fact that it was of course the place where I did my first summer season with The Nu-Notes in 1960, and of course the place where I met Ann, a 17-year-old Butlin Red Coat, whom I later married. And yes, we are still together as I write this, nearly 50 years on, not bad in this day and age. The show turned out to be a great success and everything I could have wished for. It would be very hard for me to top this at my stage in life, I was thinking. But who knows, I might still get that elusive hit record. Then of course pigs fly, don't they?

opposite 1996, Russ performing in his Rock 'n' Roll Spectacular at Butlins Bognor Regis.

above and below Russ is singing with his eight dancers during his one-hour non-stop Rock Show.

opposite Russ giving it his all during his Rock 'n' Roll spectacular, Butlins 1996.

All good things come to an end, as did my summer season. It was October 1996 and, following my last show, I have to say it was a case of where do we go from here? Cabaret will seem very ordinary now after doing such a great show all summer. Well, I have to say that, after just a week or so, I was back doing just that, cabaret, and to be honest very grateful for it, only once or twice a week, just enough to keep me involved and, of course, the money helped.

At this time I was breeding and racing greyhounds, simply as a hobby and yes, my dogs all had a wonderful life and, when retired from racing, lived with us in the house until their passing on. In fact I still have one now – she is ten years old, the last of many.

On the show biz scene, my cabaret work would continue on and off for the next eight years until 2004, after which my life was about to change. March 2004, I move to Northern Ireland! Yes, on the face of it, an odd choice, but this all happened because my son, Darren, married a girl from a place called Ballymoney, up near Coleraine. This meant my show biz career would come to a sudden halt, since I had no contacts over there. Having settled in, I was like a fish out of water and very soon realized that we had made the wrong move. This was not where I wanted to be, though on the one hand, it was great to be near to my son, his wife and my two grandchildren. But on the other hand, I had left behind everything that was part of my life, forgetting that home is where the heart is, and take it from me, that's a definite! Well, to cut a long story short, we moved back to Hayling Island in March 2006, precisely two years from the date of moving over. It was great to be back home and, in no time at all, I was doing a few shows on the south coast and it felt like I had never been away!

left Russ is kitted out and on his way to his next gig. Don Fay was Russ Sainty's agent based in Bournemouth.

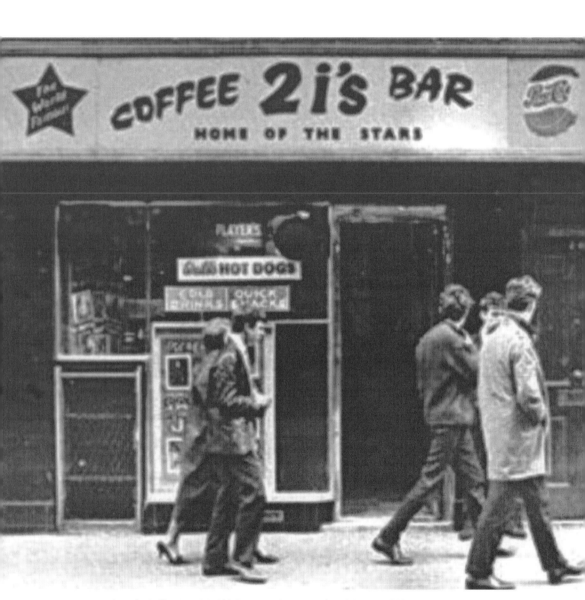

The 2 i's Coffee Bar, 59 Old Compton Street, London W1. Late 1950s.

Chapter Thirteen

A FOUNDING FATHER

I'm about to become a "Founding Father". Having only been back home for a few weeks, right out of the blue, I start to get phone calls and e-mails, all relating to my early days in show biz and my early records. I can't explain why this should happen, but it was just as though someone had switched on a light. Hey, I was not complaining, this was wonderful, I could feel this fantastic upsurge of interest in the Retro period, those heady early Rock 'n' Roll days of the late '50s, early '60s.

On 1st of August, I received an e-mail from a Mr Bob Mandry, telling me all about his project to sponsor a green, historic memorial plaque on the wall outside the 2 i's Coffee Bar, 59, Old Compton Street in London's Soho area. This, of course, being the place where myself and many other stars started their Rock 'n' Roll careers, already documented much earlier in my story. Please see copies of original e-mails and following invitation correspondence, leading up to what was just the most fantastic day, 18th September 2006. I feel sure that you my reader can imagine the excitement, apprehension and sheer delight I was feeling as our taxi slowly made its way through the crowds as we neared 59, Old Compton Street. Thankfully, there were barriers all around the premises and a few policemen about who helped get us through the crowds and into the 2 i's Coffee Bar area. It was then a case of trying to recognise each other; remember, some of us had not met up since 1958. The original owner of the Coffee Bar, Mr Paul Lincoln, was in attendance, though a little frail. Cliff Richard and The Shadows, Wee Willy Harris, Vince Eager, Bobby Brittain, Chas McDevitt, and so many more. Cliff then gave a short speech, saying how lucky he had been, and that it might have been any of us who could have made it as big as he has. Well, it was nice of Cliff to say that but personally, I think he is a credit to himself and to show business and honestly believe, whatever the circumstances, he would have been a big success.

Page 1 of 1

Subj: 2i's Coffee Bar
Date: 01/08/2006 22:53:51 GMT Standard Time
From: IMANDRY
To: Russanna60

Dear Russ,
I found this email address on the web and hope that it is still active. My name is Bob Mandry and I have been involved for the past 18 months with a project to place a plaque on 59, Old Compton Street alias the 2i's. After a long and fairly involved journey all the necessary permission has been obtained and on the 18th September this year the plaque will be unveiled by the original Wildcats. It is a very significant time as 2006 is the 50th anniversary of the opening the 2i's and, more importantly, 50 years of British Rock 'n' Roll, when Tommy Steele's 'Rocking with the Caveman' was released.
It is hoped to gather together as many of the 50s 2i's musicians as possible for the unveiling and the reception afterwards. Knowing of your connections with the 2i's I am sending, via letterpost, an official invitation from the Lord Mayor of Westminster to be present on the 18th. This will be a celebration of the true origins of British Rock music and it is unlikely that such a group of musicians will ever be able to gather together again.
Those who have accepted so far are:- Brian Locking, Jim Sullivan, Brian Bennett, Tony Belcher, Clem Cattini, Brian Gregg, Cliff, Dudley Fuller, Barney Smith, Rick Hardy, Chas McDevitt, Wee Willie Harris and Neil Christian. Invites have also been sent to Marty Wilde and Bruce Welch and they have yet to reply. I am having trouble contacting Bobby Woodman, Duffy Power and Vince Eager and if you could help with telephone numbers or addresses for these people I would be very grateful. If you also knew of any other musicians that played at the 2i's that I have not included I would very much appreciate their names and contact details so I can send them invites also. It has been my aim from the inception of this project that it will be a time when the "founding fathers" of British Rock 'n' Roll are given the true recognition for their pioneering work.
LBC radio, Capital radio, the BBC and ITV have all been contacted and it is hoped to have good coverage via the media. I was disappointed when I contacted the NME, who in September 1956 officially recognized that British Rock 'n' Roll was alive and growing, when they told they planned to do nothing about recognizing this anniversary.
I have sent the invitation to the address on the 2005 letter you wrote so I trust you are still living there and it will be received safely. I look forward to hearing from you and sincerely hope you could join us on the day I appreciate that you have some distance to travel but it would be great if we could all get together for this anniversary.
Regards,
Bob Mandry

The actual e-mail and correspondence from Bob Mandry and The Westminster City Council confirming details of the 2 i's Coffee Bar Commemorative Plaque ceremony and those of us who were invited to attend.

City of Westminster

THE RIGHT WORSHIPFUL THE LORD MAYOR OF WESTMINSTER

HAS PLEASURE IN INVITING

Russ & Ann Sainty

To attend the unveiling of a
Commemorative Green Plaque to

THE 2i'S COFFEE BAR
(1956-1970)
Birthplace of British Rock'n Roll and the popular music industry

at 59 Old Compton Street, W1

The ceremony will take place on Monday 18th September 2006

at 2.30 p.m.

RSVP   refreshments will be served
Miss Gillian M Dawson   afterwards
Manager, Green Plaques
Westminster City Council
City Hall, 64 Victoria Street
LONDON SW1A 6QP
Tel: 020 7641 2457
Fax: 020 7641 3050
e-mail : gdawson@westminster.gov.uk

sponsored by Mr Robert Mandry

2I'S COMMEMORATION PLAQUE

Westminster Chapel,
Buckingham Gate
London SW1E 6BS

11th September 2006

Dear Russ,
Please find enclosed your security pass, order of ceremony and guest list for the 2i's event next Monday.
Apart from denoting the historical significance of the site, one of the other aims in organising this event was to publicly acknowledge the contribution that this era of musicians has made to British rock music. Too often it would appear that British rock music began at the Cavern and the pioneering work done by yourselves goes largely unacknowledged. I would personally like to say thank you for the hours of enjoyment your music has given me and trust the occasion will give you a chance to reminisce and get together with colleagues you may well have not seen for many years.
It is quite likely that there will be a lot of spectator interest as well as the media present. Half the road is to be cordoned off between 2p.m. and 3p.m. with access on one lane only. There will also be no parking at all in the area around the 2i's for this period. Cars used by guests must be parked away from the area once people have alighted and then return at the end of the event to pick up their passengers.
In order to help guests who may be using public transport, particularly for the final part of the journey, I have laid on a courtesy car running a shuttle service to 59OCS from Charing Cross main line station forecourt between 1.45 p.m. & 2.30 p.m. To enable me to know how many would like to avail themselves of this service, it must be pre-booked by phoning me on 07931 764440 by Friday evening (15th).
We have to vacate the restaurant by 6.30 p.m. at the latest but that should allow a good three hours for people to relax, enjoy the reception and catch up with old colleagues. This is your day, I hope it will be a memorable one,
Regards,

Bob Mandry

Bob Mandry
Sponsor and Organiser

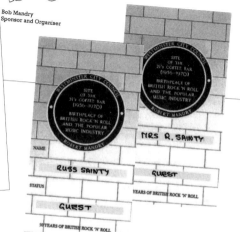

above A group photo of 2 i's coffee bar musicians and singers who performed there between 1956 and 1960. The occasion being that of the unveiling of a Green Historic Plaque on the wall outside what used to be the 2 i's Coffee Bar. Commemorating 50 years and the birth place of British Rock 'n' Roll, date 18th September 2006. Back row L to R: Brian Bennett, Tex Makin, Paul Lincoln, Bobby Woodman, Cliff Richard, John Allison, Brian (Liquorice) Locking, Neil Christian, Vince Eager, Big Jim Sullivan and Michael Fogerty. Front row L to R: Chas Mc Devitt, Ken Cook, Dudley Fuller, Rick Hardy, John Pilgrim, Wee Willie Harris, Tony Annis and Russ Sainty. *Photo courtesy of Robert Mandry*

below Russ Sainty and Cliff Richard enjoying the day.

CITY OF WESTMINSTER

SITE OF THE
2i's COFFEE BAR
(1956-1970)

BIRTHPLACE OF
BRITISH ROCK 'N ROLL
AND THE POPULAR
MUSIC INDUSTRY

ROBERT MANDRY

above A general view looking west down Old Compton Street, showing most of the invited celebs, some of the general public and an array of press photographers. Cliff can be seen left giving a short speech.

below Cliff, Russ and Wee Willie deep in conversation about those great early days at The 2 i's. Wee Willie played at the 'Cali', 1962. *Photos courtesy of Robert Mandry*

above Back row L to R: Buddy Britain, Tex Makin, Bobby Woodman, Paul Lincoln, Cliff Richard and Vince Eager. Middle row L to R: Dudley Fuller, Barney Smith, Wee Willie Harris, Neil Christian, Mike Fogerty. Front row L to R: Ken Cook, John Pilgrim, Tony Annis and Russ Sainty. *below* Back row L to R: Brian Bennett, Cliff Richard, Bruce Welch, Brian (Liquorice) Locking, Russ Sainty, with Chas Mc Devitt and Wee Willie Harris at the front. *Photos courtesy of Robert Mandry*

For me, to have been part of this whole thing is just magic, with the knowledge that finally the 2 i's Coffee Bar has been officially recognised as the birthplace of British Rock 'n' Roll, with those of us who performed there in those early days now recognised as the "Founding Fathers" of this great music. That I am a part of British Rock 'n' Roll history is more than I could ever have wished for and nobody can take it away from me. The plaque is now there for the entire world to see and well worth a visit, should you be in the area.

left Russ with Vince Eager. My, he's a big boy! Vince played at the 'Cali' of course in 1962. *below* Clem Cattini and Russ meet up again. Clem, a great drummer who has played on hundreds of hit records, but perhaps best known as drummer with The Tornadoes and their massive hit single "Telstar". They played at the 'Cali' in 1963.

left The 2 i's Coffee Bar in the late '50s/early '60s.

14 The News, Thursday, September 21, 2006

■ **MUSIC:** Hayling singer remembers his part as a founding father of modern British music

Recognition goes to rock's golden oldies

by Sofia Zagzoule
The News

A GOLDEN oldie has been reunited with one of the 'young ones'.

Singer Russ Sainty, 70, of Manor Road, Hayling Island, met up with former jam partner Sir Cliff Richard on Monday at the site of the 2i's in Old Compton Street, London.

The coffee bar opened in 1956 and became a hotbed for aspiring young stars and big-name acts of the day.

This week it was given an official commemoration plaque on its 50th anniversary in celebration and recognition of its role in founding British rock'n'roll.

Russ was one of many musicians – along with Brian Bennett, Bruce Welch, Chas McDevitt and Wee Willie Harris – to have his contribution to UK rock'n'roll officially recognised on Monday.

The sponsor and organiser of the event, Bob Mandry, said: "Too often it would appear that British rock music began at the Cavern and the pioneering work done by these musicians goes largely unacknowledged.

'This event was organised to publicly acknowledge the contribution that this era of musicians made to British rock music.'

Russ, who sang at the bar on a regular basis, was privileged to have the Shadows as his backing band on numerous occasions and to sing alongside Sir Cliff.

'I had not seen all these people for years,' he said.

'We were being hailed as the founding fathers of rock'n'roll, it was a great day.

'I used to earn about £1 a night for playing in those days, but to be honest I don't remember getting paid at all.

'But it was not a matter of money, it was the atmosphere and the people you'd meet.

'It was a very important part of history: people always think that the Cavern in Liverpool was where rock'n'roll started - but it was all at the 2i's in a dingy cellar.

'There are toilets in the new building now where we used to play.'

Russ said that Sir Cliff was tremendous, and extremely down to earth.

'He was with all the people he had started out with,' Russ said, 'so even though he was the one who made it so big he was saying that he had been the lucky one.'

sofia.zagzoule
@thenews.co.uk

Sir Cliff Richard and Russ Sainty at the site of the 2i's coffee bar, the birthplace of British rock'n'roll

SIR CLIFF RICHARD

■ Sir Cliff Richard was born Harry Webb in India on October 14, 1940.

■ As an early rock-and-roller in the late 1950s, he went on to become a successful film star – his biggest hit, Summer Holiday, was a top box office attraction in 1962.

■ Sir Cliff has been a musi-cal icon for more than four decades.

■ During his 47 years of success he has sold a staggering 250 million records.

■ He converted to Christianity in 1985.

■ His other passion after music is tennis.

■ He was knighted in 1995 for charitable works.

Following this wonderful occasion and the press coverage it had, my phone didn't stop ringing, and my e-mail in-box was red hot. Amongst all the telephone calls that I'm getting, one of them is from a lovely guy called Dell Richardson, who tells me he has been trying to catch up with me for a long time. Dell has a wonderful Rock 'n' Roll Show on Radio Caroline every Tuesday night called "Good Rockin' Tonight". It is three hours long and is live on Sky worldwide. He wanted me to be a guest on the show, and a date was fixed for 31st October 2006. Well, I have to tell you, it was a really smashing show, Dell playing all my old 45 singles, and we were getting great feed back live from all parts of the world. It was a really memorable night, I have to say, which again created more interest in one Mr Russ Sainty. Strangely enough, whilst all this is happening to me, Roger Dean, Nu-Notes guitarist, sends me a copy of a magazine called Pipeline (Instrumental Review) and on the front cover is a great picture of The Nu-Notes. Inside, even better. A great write-up on the group and myself and, best of all for me, was the fact that this well regarded magazine stated, and I quote, "One of the regular discs on that auto-changer was The Nu-Notes' 'Fury'. Its frantic tempo and dazzling guitar sounds place it in the elite of UK classics, up there with The Cougars' 'Saturday Night at the Duck Pond', The Hunters' 'The Storm' and The Fentones' 'The Mexican' amongst the Royalty of British '60s instrumentals. So it is with great pleasure that we finally reveal a little of the history behind the record." End of quote. Why should this excite me so much? Answer, "Fury was composed by none other than Russ Sainty." Yes indeed, and I'm extremely proud of the fact that this number should be regarded in this way. Wow! Rock On!

I'm still baffled as to why all this interest in Russ Sainty and The Nu-Notes in the year 2006. I'm told by many Rock 'n' Roll enthusiasts that there really is a great interest in early Rock 'n' Roll groups and their music because it was real, it was original. We gave a performance when recording, as against today when everything and every word on a record is manufactured, computerised, analysed etc., etc., and perhaps originals are always better than copies?

2007, A YEAR OF CELEBRATION!

Well, perhaps not every day, but through this year, whenever I do a show, it will be celebration time. And why not, this is my FIFTY YEARS IN SHOW BIZ, 1957–2007 and still rockin'! It's been a busy year, with cabaret bookings for Warner Holidays and other holiday centres along the South Coast. I'm also booked to do a summer season for New Horizon, starting in May; so all in all,

THAT WAS THEN JULY **1983**

Saturday, April 14, 2007

WIN DRINK EAT PLAY EXPLORE WATCH ENJOY

Weekend The News

ROCK'N'ROLL MEMORIES

1950s star Russ Sainty, from Hayling Island, recalls a new single he launched in 1983 in a bid for chart success. RACHEL JONES reports

"Sometimes I feel like slipping away from it all, but after a week or two I'm ready for work again. It's not that I'm ambitious. It's more like Magnus Magnusson says to contestants on 'Mastermind' . . . I've started so I'll finish."

● David Essex: Can't wait tomorrow.

Russ brings back the 50s classics

Hayling rock 'n' roller Russ Sainty has sold his £90,000 house in a dramatic bid to re-launch his musical career.

He used some of the money to make a new single, "The 50s Hits Right Here on 45," which is already getting extensive airplay.

It contains a succession of classic 50s tracks in the "Stars on 45" style.

He still talks fondly of knocking around with Cliff Richard, Tommy Steele, and Marty Wilde in London's famous 2 Is Coffee Bar during early days of rock 'n' roll.

Since then he has worked some success on the cabaret trade. Of the single he says: "There is a big market for these songs of the which really are today's nostalgia.

"The young kids love these songs too, they're so fresh, happy and harmless."

Rock'n'roller Russ Sainty made another bid for chart success in July, 1983, when he made a new single *The 50s Hits Right Here On 45*.

The 1850s star, who was a hit with his band The Nu-Notes, realised there was a big market for nostalgia and teamed up with a contact in the music industry to record the new single – a succession of classic 50s tracks in the *Stars On 45* style.

Some of the proceeds came from the sale of the Hayling Island singer's home and for a while it looked like all the effort would be worth it.

Now 70 and still living on Hayling Island, Russ says: 'It was getting loads of airplay and, having had quite a few knocks in my career, I thought this was the one that was going to make it.

'But it wasn't distributed, it got left in a warehouse. It didn't end up in the shops and I ended up with thousands of records, but I've been doing cabaret for years, and sold some through that.'

But he can laugh about it now. 'I still have some now. I was on a Radio Caroline show recently and gave some away. I'm getting rid of them but you could say it's taking a bit of time. Still, at least I've got plenty of copies for myself. If I ever want to listen to it, no problem.'

Russ was a big name in the 1950s. One of the original rock'n'rollers, he used to hang around with Cliff Richard, Tommy Steele and Marty Wilde in London's famous 2is cafe bar.

Recently he teamed up with Cliff Richard and other stars of the era to unveil a plaque in London marking the site of the bar.

Despite the fact he prefers the quiet life of Hayling Island to the hustle and bustle of London, he is as enthusiastic about his music as ever. Since 1983, Russ has been extremely busy – working as a holiday camp entertainments manager in the 1980s and starring on the cabaret circuit. He's still a big hit on stage and has no thoughts of retiring.

'I can't stand the word retire. I'm 70 but you wouldn't know it. I still have plenty of energy and I've no plans to give any of it up.

People love 50s music. It has many fans around the world, including a lot of young people. And I don't mean a passing interest – a lot of them are into it in a big way.'

The music industry is famously fickle, but Russ still has a lot of fans and a b-side instrumental he wrote – *Fury* – is now being hailed as a classic of the era in music magazines.

He lives with his wife, Ann, a former Butlins Redcoat, and for the past three years has been busy writing his life story. The couple have two grown-up children and three grandchildren.

■ Russ Sainty points to the plaque in memory of the 2is cafe

■ Russ Sainty: Kids love these songs

CITY OF WESTMINSTER

SITE OF THE 2i's COFFEE BAR (1956–1970)

BIRTHPLACE OF BRITISH ROCK 'N ROLL AND THE POPULAR MUSIC INDUSTRY

ROBERT MANDRY

WERE YOU IN THE HEADLINES?

■ Were you in *The News* headlines any time up until 1992?

We'd love to hear your memories and find out what's happened to you since. Contact Rachel Jones on (023) 9262 2160 or e-mail her at rachel.jones@thenews.co.uk with details of the story, the date it appeared and your daytime phone number.

If today's memories have got you thinking, please get in touch with your own reminiscences from that period. Each week we'll be featuring reader feedback.

And don't forget to read our nostalgia correspondent Bob Hind's *Way We Were* page on Monday, plus his daily columns from Tuesday to Friday.

things are going along very sweetly for me at this time. I am of course almost at journey's end with regard to my Cali Story and my show biz life after, but I did promise you a special "Cali Surprise". So let me explain all without further delay. During the year of 2005, while I was living in Northern Ireland, I had an e-mail from Jaybee, the webmaster of the California Ballroom Web Site, and she was able to give me a telephone number of someone I hadn't seen since the year 1965 at the 'Cali'. She was the young lady who, together with myself and Ronnie Carroll, was singing at the 'Cali''s opening night 12th March 1960, with The Ray Miller Orchestra. Her name was Edwina Green. She, of course, being a daughter of Mr and Mrs Green, the owners of the 'Cali'.

Now, as I've mentioned before, being booked so many times during my six years at the 'Cali', I did feel very close to the entire Green family, not forgetting Little Dennis, who was not a family member.

Well, I made a call to Edwina and she just could not believe it was me on the other end. We talked for about an hour until my ear was sore, and I'm sure she felt the same. After this call, we did keep in contact and, only this year, I was lucky enough to meet up with her for the first time in 42 years. No, she hadn't changed a bit, we just seemed to carry on like brother and sister, chatting about those wonderful Cali days like it was only yesterday, living proof that my links with the California Ballroom will never fade away, nor should they. My time spent there meant so much to me in many different ways and the memories live on, and on and on and on and on!

A photo taken in the summer of 2007 showing myself with Edwina Green, now Hillier, on the left, and right is the California website master known as Jaybee. Yes, we were having a party!

FUNNY STORIES

RUSS HITS THE DECK

Now, as you can imagine, over the past 50 years that I've been in the biz, as the saying goes, there have been hundreds of funny things happen. They simply come and they go and that's the end of it. However, I must mention a few, the first one of which happened to me personally.

I was booked for a week's cabaret supporting Freddy and the Dreamers up in the Lake District at a place called Whitehaven, and the club was called The Zodiac Club. After rehearsing with the band on my arrival, I was recommended some "Show Biz Digs" bed and breakfast. I had to drive out of town about six miles back into the countryside, where I found the place, a lovely big farm house. I booked in and the lady of the house told me that The Dreamers were also staying at the house. Well, a few days went by and everything was spot on. The lady would leave plenty of sandwiches for us all to have a bit of supper after the show, but she and her husband were always in bed by the time we arrived at the house at about midnight. Well, you can imagine the banter between us lads, and it would sometimes be 3am before we made our way to bed. However, on the Wednesday night, at about 2.30am, I said my goodnights to all The Dreamers and made my way up a very steep old staircase, carrying my stage clothes in one hand and my small suitcase in the other. As I reached the top step, I somehow tripped and fell straight into a door across the hallway opposite the staircase, and this all happened in absolute pitch black. There was not a glimmer of light from anywhere and the noise was just horrific, as you may well imagine. Well, the door must have been closed tight, because I hit it very hard, so much so I broke the latch and the door flew wide open and I was in a heap on the floor, Oh dear, it just happened to be the property owners' bedroom! I yelled out,

"I'm so sorry – it's me – I'm not drunk. No, I'm not drunk, I just tripped!" As I lay prostrate on the bedroom floor with my stage clothes wrapped around my neck, I hear the lady of the house screaming, and the man by now had jumped out of bed thinking it was a burglar who had made a mistake. Eventually, with me still shouting out, "It's me, Russ," over and over again, someone switched on a light and, I can tell you, it was not a pretty sight. With me spread-eagled on the floor, the man was standing over me in his long johns (it was winter), and the lady of the house was still in bed hiding beneath the sheets! This was my most embarrassing incident without doubt and something which the next morning gave us all the biggest laugh, as we discussed what happened; something those of us involved will never forget!

THE COMIC AND THE BRANDY BOTTLE

It's around 1974 and I'm away from home doing three weeks cabaret in the Northern Clubs. I'm in "pro digs" (B and B) with about four other acts, all working the same area as myself. During the day we would all exchange stories and general chit-chat, and one quite well known act of the day told me this story, which he swears is true.

A very well known comedian (a household name in the '70s), who has now passed on, was in digs in the North of England, and the lady of the house, who had lost her husband, took a shine to this comic, so much so that by the Thursday of his one week stay, bed and breakfast, just before leaving for his gig at around 7pm, she went to her sideboard and brought out an unopened bottle of brandy. She said to the comic (who shall remain nameless) "Let's have a nice glass of brandy before you go to the club." Well, after two large brandys the comic gives her a peck on the cheek and gets ready to leave for work, when the lady of the house told him she would not be in tomorrow until late, so would see him on Saturday in order for him to pay his bill.

Well, the next day (Friday), before leaving for his club gig, he decided to find the bottle of brandy and help himself. By now, the bottle was down to very little. He then panicked and decided that since he was leaving the property the next day (Saturday evening), he would top up the brandy bottle in order that it would not notice. By now he was a little merry, so decided to "pee" in the bottle, bringing it back to the original amount, great! Job done, she'll never notice a thing. It's now Saturday evening and he calls the lady of the house in order to pay his B and B bill for the week and whilst doing just that, the lady said to him, "You must have a nice glass of brandy before you go and I'll join you." Ouch! Whatever happened next we shall never know, but at a guess I would say he suddenly became a non drinker and got out of the house a bit sharpish!

"MAX AND JIMMY"

This is another true story that happened to a very good friend of mine, a musician, singer/comedian, whose name is David Brown – in his own words.

I worked with the great Max Wall at the Pier Theatre, Cleethorpes, back in the '70s. It was a time when Max was making a comeback. One night after the show, we both ended up in a night club. After a lengthy conversation and several glasses of alcohol, we were asked to leave as the club was closing. The combination of drink and "one to one" with a legend was almost too much for me, it was just magic. We continued talking as Max was propped against a street lamp post that cast an amber pool of light around him. I was still running off at the mouth, telling Max about the early days, when as a young boy with my grandparents I had listened to him on the radio and later seen him on TV. As I rambled on, he looked like he was in a trance, barely able to stand and doubtless grateful for the lamp post. Then I mentioned another great, the comedian Jimmy Wheeler, even attempting his catchphrase, "Aye aye...That's your lot!" Suddenly Max opened his eyes and in that wonderful deep voice with puckered lips he drawled, "It's a shame about Jimmy."

I said, "Why?"

Max slurred, "He drinks!"

I found the moment so amusing, and the whole thing quite bizarre. I started laughing as Max was being collected and driven away. Oh, great memories!

DISCOGRAPHY

RUSS SAINTY AND THE NU-NOTES
Singles

A Side	B Side	Label	Year
Happy Go Lucky Me	Standing Around	Top Rank JAR 381	1960
Too Shy	Race With The Devil	Decca 45 F11270	1960
Don 't Believe Him Donna	Your Other Love	Decca 45 11325	1961
Keep Your Love Locked	I've Got A Girl	HMV POP 1055	1962
Send Me The Pillow That You Dream On	What Do You Know About That	HMV POP 1069	1962
Unforgettable Love	The Twinkle In Your Eye	HMV POP 1181	1963
Lonesome Town	That's How I'm Gonna Love You	Parlophone R 5168	1964
This Is My Lovely Day	Bless You Girl	Columbia DB 7397	1964
She	Saving My Tears	Columbia DB 7708	1965
It Ain 't That Easy	And Then	Columbia DB 7521	1965
We're Falling In Love	I Can Give You A Love	Rediffusion RIM 8	1968
The 50s Hits Right Here On 45		Russ Records Russ 1	1983
Too Much	One of These Mornings	HMV R 005/6	1959

A private single for The 59 Club, Eton Mission, Hackney, East London

A Side	B Side	Label	Year
Last Night Was Made For Love	As You Like It	Embassy WB 509	1961

Under name Johnny Chester

Albums

Title	Label	Year
Million Sellers made famous by The Beatles *Sung by RUSS SAINTY*	Boulevard 4064	1966
The Genius of Lennon & McCartney *Sung by RUSS SAINTY*	Society ST SOC 1035	1967
Swinging London *Sung by RUSS SAINTY*	Boulevard 4070	1972
A Pot of Pure Gold *Sung by RUSS SAINTY & THE DALLAS BOYS*	President 5017447511414	1991
UK Teenage Jamboree *Various artistes, includes "Race with the Devil"*	?	?
Legends of British Rock 'n' Roll *includes "Race with the Devil"*	CD ECD 3406	?
Rockin' the British Isles *Various artistes, includes "Don't Believe Him Donna"*	RRR 1003 Australian Pressing	?
CD Something Tells Me *Sung by RUSS SAINTY*	President 574	Early 1970s

Go Away Little Girl
Cinebox Films 1960s version of our music videos today, they were played on The Cinebox Jukebox and cost one shilling a play

THE NU-NOTES
Instrumental Singles

A Side	B Side	Label	Year
Walk Don't Run *under name Rhet Stoller*	All Rhet	Decca 45-F 11271	1960
Chariot *under name Rhet Stoller*	Night Theme	Decca 45-F11302	1960
Hall of Mirrors	Fury	HMV POP 1232	1963
Kathy	Sunset	HMV POP 1311	1964

Instrumental Albums

A Side	B Side	Label	Year
Instrumental Diamonds 1 *Various artistes*		?	?
Jumpin', British Instrumentals *Various artistes*		Sequel NEXCD 149	?

THE NU-NOTES Personnel
There were various changes over the years

Name	Instrument and order of joining
Rhet Stoller	Guitar (1)
Roy Toft	Guitar/Vocals
Mel Miller	Bass/Vocals
Laurie Jay	Drums (1)
Bernie Martin	Drums (2 & 4)
Big Jim Sullivan	Guitar (2)
Roger Dean	Guitar (3)
Nigel Menday	Drums (3)

Some useful and relevant websites

www.russsainty.com	Russ Sainty
www.californiaballroom.info	The official 'Cali' website. Webmaster "Jaybee"
www.cali-r.com	Reunion events, particularly '70s soul. Promoter Sid Hudson.
www.rogerdean.info	Roger Dean (The Nu-Notes)

Keywords: Russ Sainty and 2 i's Coffee Bar

LETTERS FROM VARIOUS PERFORMERS, 2007

FROM BERNIE MARTIN, DRUMMER WITH RUSS SAINTY AND THE NU-NOTES (1959–1965 WITH A SHORT BREAK IN 1962)

My memories, if I wrote them all down, would be endless. It all began for me, on a cold winter's day in 1959; I joined my first professional group, Russ Sainty and The Nu-Notes. I can even recall the very first song we rehearsed, a little ditty called "Travelling Light", a hit for Cliff Richard. I soon got to know the guys pretty quick. Russ was a rather "calm" sort of person; Roy Toft, our rhythm guitarist, was outspoken and a very confident person; Mel Miller, the bass player, was also outspoken, and a bit crazy, always having a laugh with everyone – he played the double bass when I joined but soon changed to a Fender electric guitar. Rhet Stoller, our lead guitarist, was very enthusiastic and would be up day and night creating new sounds and arranging new numbers for the group; he was also very spoilt by his parents, who would do anything and go anywhere for him, a brilliant guitarist for all that! After a year or so, Rhet left The Nu-Notes to concentrate on recording and composing, and we were joined by another brilliant guitarist for a short time, whose name was Big Jim Sullivan. Following Jim's departure from the group, we were finally joined by Roger Dean, a rather quiet person at first, but he soon became one of the group's personalities, and his lead guitar work was outstanding. I remember so well doing my first BBC broadcast with Russ and The Group; it was Saturday Club, and the producer was Jimmy Grant, and compered by Brian Matthew. When I first joined Russ Sainty and The Nu-Notes, we were doing regular weekend bookings for all the American air bases in the south of England, but in 1960 we did a gig in Dunstable, a very large ballroom called the California Pool Ballroom. During the summer of 1960 we did a Butlins season at Bognor Regis, and in the autumn we were soon back at the 'Cali', as we soon called the place. This would lead to us gigging at this ballroom on a regular basis, and we very soon had a fantastic following in the area. Most weeks we would be top of the bill, even when The Rolling Stones appeared! I have great memories of the place, and why not? We played there for six years, and never did we have a bad night.

Yes, I did have a short spell playing the 'Cali' with Rhet Stoller, and we backed people like Jess Conrad and Terry Dean, but this period was short lived and I rejoined The Nu-Notes, and Rhet went back to recording in his basement studio, composing and recording the football anthem "Match of The Day", oh boy what a hit!

We were a great outfit, and could "rave" as good as anyone, but we could also play very refined music, as demonstrated with our EMI recording of the instrumental called "Kathy" composed by Mel Miller, our bass player. I could go on and on, so many wonderful memories of my days playing at the fabulous California Ballroom. Oh Happy days, how I wish we could do it all over again!

Bernie Martin

FROM ROGER DEAN, LEAD GUITAR WITH RUSS SAINTY AND THE NU-NOTES (1962–1965)

I first met Russ in 1962. I had been taking a lunch break from my day job at 'Maples', the West End furnishing emporium, and had nipped down to Charing Cross Road to have a look at the guitars... although I couldn't afford to actually buy one, the guys in the store didn't know that, so I was happily showing off my technique (very basic!) in Lew Davis' guitar store.

I became aware of a presence behind me, which was Russ. To cut a long story short, he invited me down to see a 'Russ Sainty and The Nu-Notes' performance at a dancehall in Leicester Square. I thought that the band were fantastic. Having seen all the rock 'n' roll shows at the Slough 'Adelphi', and having imagined myself to be a pro. musician on many occasions... I jumped at the chance to play with them the very next Saturday at the California Ballroom in Dunstable.

What I didn't realise at that time was that I was replacing two of the best guitar players in the country... Rhet Stoller and Big Jim Sullivan. If I'd realised the enormity of stepping into their shoes, I might have fought shy of being available on that night... but as things have turned out, I shall always be grateful to Russ, Mel, Roy, Bernie, and Nigel Menday (drummer in 1962) for giving me a break in a career that spanned forty six years, and has taken me around the world twelve times, including a 'Royal Variety Performance' with the Joe Loss Orchestra.

I have so many memories of our time at the 'Cali', so it would be impossible to list them. I suppose a couple would be the night the Rolling Stones played the Interval Band spot on the little stage, while we were the stars on the main stage. Another outstanding night would have been Johnny Kidd and the Pirates ... that Mick Green was some guitar player, even in those early '60s days! Another great band was the Flintstones, with Rod Freeman on guitar.

Mr Green and his daughter Edwina always made us feel welcome, in fact for us it virtually was home... we played there so many times we should have taken camp beds and lived there! I often wonder what happened to Dennis, who was always on hand to help us with any problems.

Well, that's about all I have to say... except thanks again Russ, you saved me from a life of doom selling bits of wood to people with (usually) wood between the ears!

Best Always, Roger Dean

FROM CRAIG DOUGLAS

Russ has been a good friend of mine for a long long time, and I always have plenty of fun and laughter when in his company. We first met in the year 1960 at the California (Pool) Ballroom in Dunstable, when his group The Nu-Notes gave me a superb backing. Russ went on to perform well over 300 sessions at this wonderful venue, wow! That's some going!

In the autumn of 1960 I joined Russ and The Nu-Notes, who were booked to do a country wide tour, with myself topping the bill, The Mudlarks, The Avons, Al Saxon, and Alan (fluff) Freeman. It was a super tour, promoted by my agent, Bunny Lewis, which turned out to be a great success.

It was very clear to me at this time that Russ Sainty was a bit special; he was able to sing heavy rock, and even better, a big ballad, In fact Russ made some cracking singles, but for one reason or another, didn't quite hit the jackpot, "Send Me The Pillow That You Dream On" being one of his best sellers in 1962.

During the 47 years that Russ and I have been good buddies, I have visited and stayed with him and Ann his wife and they have always made me so welcome. In the early '70s, I recall visiting Russ at a wonderful new house he had built on Hayling Island in Hampshire; he can turn his hand to almost anything and has done so much during his life, something I've always admired; unlike myself – I'm a bit "ham fisted".

In the late eighties, Russ suddenly went to the dogs! No not literally you understand, but he got into breeding and racing greyhounds, simply as a hobby, Russ being an avid dog lover, who gave his dogs the five star treatment from birth until they ended their days. Through all the different business ventures Russ has been involved with, he has never stopped performing and in truth, he is singing better than ever in this, his 50th year in show business, having started at the famous 2 i's Coffee Bar in London's Soho in August 1957, proof indeed, that you don't need hit records if you're good enough and take it from me, Russ is. They say that behind every successful man is a woman and none better than Ann; she, together with daughter Michelle and son Darren, has always been there with support and encouragement for Russ to further his career. This life story is yet another achievement and tells it all. To conclude, I want to say that Russ Sainty is a shining example of all the best in mankind, a true friend, a great performer, and "Almost a Rock 'n' Roll Legend".

Craig Douglas

FROM MEL MILLER, DOUBLE BASE, BASE GUITAR AND VOCALS WITH RUSS SAINTY AND THE NU-NOTES (1959–1965)

Show Business for me was a truly wonderful experience, especially being part of a terrific group, Russ Sainty and The Nu-Notes. I am Mel Miller, sometimes affectionately known as "Mad Mel", since I was always "The Zany One".

Although we performed at thousands of venues all around the country and abroad, some of my best memories were when performing at the California Ballroom in Dunstable. For example, falling through the stage one night! Everyone thought it was part of our act, but it was for real and I still have the scar on my shin to prove it! How then could I ever forget the 'Cali'!

Russ was a great guy to work with in those heady Rock 'n' Roll times, completely professional, dedicated to keeping the highest standards and he would have us rehearsing at every spare moment. We became a group's group; many of the groups who became household names looked up to us and would emulate what we were doing, and I for one am very proud of that. This fact is confirmed even more so, when you consider that we as a group probably did more BBC Broadcasts during the early sixties than any other group of our type; we really were favourites with the Beeb!

All the years I've known Russ we have never fallen out. I do however recall one night at the 'Cali', Russ had a right go at me, but I deserved it. I was late on stage, because I had been snogging a pretty girl outside the ballroom. Oh Dear! It was of course all part of the fun and growing up, and those wonderful Cali memories will stay with me forever. I am still in contact with Russ and the other guys of The Nu-Notes, with the exception of Rhet Stoller, who seems to be a recluse, and of course our rhythm guitarist and vocalist, Roy Toft, who sadly passed away in 2003; we all remember Roy with great affection.

Though we didn't have a number one hit record, it's life's experience that's important, and nobody can ever take that away! So Three Cheers for THE CALI, never to be forgotten!

Mel Miller

FROM BRIAN POOLE OF THE TREMELOES

When asked to write a small piece by my good friend Russ Sainty about the California Ballroom years, I jumped at the chance to try to explain the importance of the live music scene and its part in the massive move in music from the big bands and solo artistes to popular groups of three to five musicians and singers.

Also a chance to give some long overdue praise to certain bands, that, although they did not have the massive chart hits, were and are still the best respected acts of our time, with many fans still supporting their music.

The Tremeloes and I started our band in the late fifties, listening to Lonnie Donegan and, if we could find him on our radios, Buddy Holly, with a little Louis Jordan and Nellie Lutcher on the side. We started recording in 1961–1962 and by then had formed ourselves into a professional vocal and instrumental group.

A photo taken at London's Dorchester Hotel, summer 2007, showing Russ Sainty, Craig Douglas and Brian Poole, and yes we all played at the 'Cali'!

Looking back to the California makes me remember that without Russ Sainty and the Nu-Notes, Rob Storm and the Whispers, Nero and the Gladiators, Keith Kelly and Mike Berry and the Outlaws, things could have been different for us. While we were up in Liverpool and other places North of Watford, there was a great live music scene going on right on our doorstep, rocking the Dunstable Downs on quite a few occasions, remarking to each other that it was not good enough to just play and sing the music any more; they, or in particular Russ, were using showmanship with great success. This was the way to go. By 1963, we were No.1 in the charts and were ready to play at the California Dunstable.

We played there four or five times, usually on hot nights and so using the pool after the show with great glee. Eddy Green and Russ were right. Make a show of it. That's where the great '60s live scene in the South was started.

Meeting Russ again after many years was a great pleasure. He still looks great (Bastard!) and remembers all about the California Ballroom which he not only opened but successfully played at many times watched by a few Tremeloes.

This is a pleasure Russ and it's nice to know that you also remember us with kindness.

Brian Poole

FROM PETER LANGFORD, GUITAR AND VOCALS WITH THE BARRON KNIGHTS

That very special day, 12th August 1960 will always be a wonderful memory for the Barron Knights.

It was our first show at the California Ballroom Dunstable and probably one of the most important shows in the history of our group. Because we were local lads from Leighton Buzzard seven miles away and trying desperately to make a name for ourselves, we couldn't believe such a big venue was so close. Mr Green, the owner, had heard about us and very kindly gave us the above date. We soon ran around every street, youth club, pub etc and told everybody we knew, and it worked because on that special night it was packed with folks from Leighton Buzzard.

The group on with us was Russ Sainty and the Nu-Notes and the first group we had ever worked alongside. We couldn't believe the standard of their singing and musicianship. Russ had all the ladies right where he wanted them and he sang like I wish I could. Rhet Stoller played guitar great and made the whole ballroom gather round the stage while he played "Caravan", sitting down. I learned so much from Russ and the boys and it made me go home and work even harder on my playing as well as raising the standard of our show.

We soon became regulars at the 'Cali' and made great friends with Russ, 'cos he was always there doing such a great job singing exactly what the crowd wanted.

The list of the acts that came to perform is endless – Cliff Bennett, Roy Castle, Dusty Springfield, Eric Clapton, Stevie Wonder, etc etc etc it goes on and on.

Even to this day we get the same thing said to us.

I think one of the magic nights for us was the night we had our first hit record "Call up The Groups". We went to do the famous TV show 'Ready Steady Go', then rushed from London to do our spot at the 'Cali'. They were hanging from the rafters and queuing hundreds of yards to get in. When we went on stage the atmosphere was electric and the show will never be forgotten.

Yes, for sure we will never forget how important the California Ballroom was to the Barron Knights and it was Russ Sainty and The Nu-Notes who gave us a standard to match. I hope we did and if I pass where the ballroom used to be, I look to the sky and say thank you to Mr Green for the 12th August 1960.

Peter Langford

FROM MIKE BERRY

Glad you're doing ok.

I really can't remember even doing the Cali? In fact I can hardly remember what I did yesterday! I remember you in a very smart suit and with very well groomed blond hair. I also remember you throwing pillows at the audience on some tour or other!!! That's it! If you can get a page out of that, then GOOD LUCK!!!

350 spots at THE CALI.?????? F—in' 'ell!!! You deserve a medal let alone congratulations! That must have been like having a day job?!!

Don't think this'll stretch to a whole page though, do you? Good luck with the book anyway,

Cheers, Mike Berry

Russ and Gary Mills meet up again in 2007; press cutting shows the two meeting in 1963 when Gary and Russ worked together in Dagenham Essex. Gary had a massive hit with "Look For A Star" and also appeared at the 'Cali' in 1961.

Pop singer Garry Mills (left) and Russ Sainty, who made a one-night stand at Dagenham's Royal Oak Hotel on Wednesday, accompanied by the New Notes. Russ, a veteran of Saturday Club, Twistin' Time and Ring a Ding Ding, was described by the management as "fabulous." Garry has one of his records "Top Teen Baby" in the Indian hit parade. Photo: Bernard Jones.

Russ meeting up with old pal Mike Sarne, 2007, "Come Outside". Mike played at the 'Cali' in 1962. Note how tall Mike is.

SAINTY ON STARS

Just when I had completed what I thought was the last paragraph of text for this book, my publisher suggested to me that, having worked alongside and met countless numbers of Stars during my past fifty years in show business, it would be both interesting and fun to get my personal view and insight on them. "What, all of them?" I shouted! "No, No," was the reply, "just a few of them." Well, from the outset I have to sort out that word Star, which kinda makes me feel a little uncomfortable, so in an attempt to qualify it, let's say that some performers become more well known than others, be it through Television, Radio, or having Hit records etc. etc. This in turn brings popularity in the general public's eye; you become what we all know as a Star. So, in a nutshell, if you have talent and get good exposure, it should follow that you will become a Star, but as we all know there are many great talents, who for one reason or another, don't or can't get media exposure and never reach those heady heights of Stardom. On the other hand, there are some, who with very little talent, through one reason or another, do get media exposure and make those dizzy heights. Truth is that staying power and lady luck play a massive part in this little game of Stardom. So many so called Stars sometimes very quickly burn out, but I believe the real ones stay the course. Well, having got that off my chest, let's get down to business and start with some early Stars, but in no particular order.

ALMA COGAN

I first met Alma at an EMI Records Ltd. Christmas party in 1962. She was a very big star of mid '50s and early '60s and I have to say, a really nice and very attractive lady, with a great bubbly personality and a unique singing voice; for me it was love at first sight, or perhaps instant infatuation, though I'm quite certain this was not the case as far as she was concerned. She invited me to go and see her in cabaret at a military base in Essex, where she did a super show, as I recall. This was the last time I saw Miss Cogan; very sadly she passed away some years later in 1966 at a very young age of 34 years.

ARTHUR ASKEY

Comedian, film and recording Star, performing during the 1930s through until the late 1970s. Arthur was of course perhaps best known for all his hundreds of BBC Radio Shows during and after the Second World War. I was lucky enough to meet Arthur at BBC Broadcasting house in London. We were both doing different shows at the time, and of all the places to meet him it just happened to be the gents' toilets! Arthur came waltzing in and shouted to me and another person, "Hello Playmates," to which I replied "Hello Arthur, nice to meet you," giggling as I said it. Arthur then said to me, "I'm told that this is where all the big knobs hang out," laughing as he spoke to me. I then gave a quick reply, saying "Yes Arthur, but not in your case!" Arthur was of course only five foot tall! Arthur had a little chuckle to himself and replied, "I do the jokes, I thank you." Arthur was of course famous for the sayings "Hello Playmates" and "I Thank You". I never ever met Arthur Askey again, that was it, a very brief but funny meeting in the BBC toilets. Arthur, who was a Liverpudlian, sadly passed away in the year 1982.

RUSS CONWAY

A great favourite, making several big hit records during the early sixties with his magic touch on the old Joanna. I met Russ at an EMI Ltd. Friday Night Spectacular Show, in late 1962, which we used to record at Manchester Square London for Radio Luxembourg. He was not only a great talent with good looks (the ladies loved him), he was also a very very nice person, though I believe he was a little nervous and insecure when performing on stage, then aren't we all? Russ and I got chatting about songs that both he and myself had composed, and this led to Russ asking me over to his home at Mill Hill North London, suggesting we try and compose something together. Well, a week or two later, a date was arranged and over to his home I went. Within minutes of my arrival, following a glass of champagne he started to try out various melodies on the piano, as I sat trying to find first a title and then words to follow. We did eventually come up with a great number, which he suggested might be perfect for a well known singer called Dorothy Squires; it was a very big ballad, not really suitable for me. This turned out to be a one off meeting, but we did chat on the phone very often, and he would always insist on me using his real name, Trevor, and likewise calling me by my real name, Alfie. Russ Conway, who later lived at Eastbourne on the south coast, passed away in the year 2000, leaving us with some great melodies like "Side Saddle", "Roulette", "Party Pops Medley", "Always You and Me", to name but a few.

DOROTHY SQUIRES

A very well known singer from South Wales, being most popular in the 1940s and '50s and marrying Roger Moore no less, in 1953. I first met this feisty lady at her home in Kent in 1963, where she was staging a very big Charity

Garden Party with various stalls all around the grounds, finishing off with a concert in the evening, held on her patio. I recall Frank Ifield and Dorothy were the principal performers. Of course, "The Saint", Roger Moore, had left Dorothy Squires in 1961 – though she was so bitter about his leaving for another woman she would not grant Roger a divorce; this went on for many years! It was at this Charity Party that I had a chance to discuss the possibility of Ms Squires recording the song that Russ Conway and I had composed. Sadly, Dorothy Squires passed away in 1998.

VERA LYNN

Affectionately known as "The Forces Sweetheart" a massive star, who was loved by just about everyone through the Second World War with hit songs like "We'll Meet Again" and "The White Cliffs of Dover" – songs which surely helped our armed forces and indeed the nation as a whole to lift their spirits and morale during those six years of wartime. I met Vera in 1962 when Russ Sainty and The Nu-Notes were booked by the BBC to do a live broadcast of a show called "Twenties to the Twist". This was at a time when American singer Chubby Checker had made the twist a massive hit record, followed by a dance of the same name. The BBC wanted the show to cover all styles of music from the 1920s until the current day, hence the show title. Well, Vera Lynn rehearsed a few old songs, after which it was our turn to rehearse, and of course the producer had asked us to do, amongst other numbers, "The Twist". Sadly, I have to be honest and tell you that Vera Lynn sat directly in front of us and put her fingers in her ears throughout the whole song. Oh dear, we were all shocked at this display of discomfort. Why would someone we all held in very high esteem do such a thing, especially when she knew exactly what the show was all about, and believe me, we were only allowed to play very softly when broadcasting for the Beeb, and we were not a "crash bang wallop group". Oh well, perhaps Vera had her reasons, let's give her the benefit of any doubt, she is now a Dame after all.

MATT MONRO

I first met Matt whilst recording an "Easy Beat" show for the Beeb, at the Playhouse Theatre, London during the early sixties. However, some years later, we would meet up again, but this time with his wife, son Matthew and daughter Michelle. It was the year 1982; the Monro family joined the cruise ship Amerikanis, as guests of my cruise director, Derek Dean. Yes, I was booked on this ship for a nine months contract, as you may recall in my earlier text. We were sailing out of Miami Florida to The Bahamas twice weekly. With Matt and family on board, I very soon got to know them all very well, and I have to say Matt was such a generous man in all respects. He would watch our shows and say how much he loved what I was doing; equally when we were a-shore eating at a restaurant he would insist on paying for the meal. More than that, of course, he was a world star, a great singer with a wonderful voice. I recall one night on the ship, he was asked to do a song, and he decided on the number "Michelle" and as he started his voice cracked. Matt just laughed and made a joke of it, he was human after all. On another night, I recall getting drunk with son Matthew and daughter Michelle, and staying up all night, just larking about and having a giggle, oh happy days. Matt Monro died in 1985, but thankfully we are left with some wonderful recordings of songs like "Portrait Of My Love", "My Kinda Girl", "Born Free", "This Is The Life" and so many more... just listen and enjoy!

FRANK IFIELD

Having been born in England, Frank spent his young days in Australia, returning to England in 1959. In the year 1960, Frank Ifield and Russ Sainty and The Nu-Notes both recorded the same song, which for me was my first record release; it was called "Happy Go Lucky Me". As things turned out, neither of our singles did that well, but it was because of this that Frank and I got to recognise each other. I went to see him performing on a couple of occasions and of course we met again at the Dorothy Squires garden party. 1962/3 was a big time for Frank with no less than three massive hits, "I Remember You", "Lovesick Blues", "Wayward Wind" and not forgetting "Confessin'". At around this time, I recall running a competition in my Fan Club and I had to come up with a nice prize for the winner. I decided to contact Frank, who was then doing a season at the London Palladium, telling him about this, and that I had come up with an idea. I would take the winner to see the show at The Palladium, and would he be kind enough to meet the winner backstage, after which we would go for a nice meal in the nearby up market restaurant of its day, in Regent Street, called "Verries"? Frank kindly agreed to this, and on the night when we went to his dressing room, he presented the winner, a very sweet young lady from the East End of London, with a lovely bouquet of flowers. My thanks to Frank, a real star!

CLIFF RICHARD and THE SHADOWS

OK, now we are talking of people who to me feel just like family, having first met them all in 1958 at the 2 i's Coffee Bar in London. They were then, of course, The Drifters, and on many occasion would jump up on the tiny stage at the 2 i's and give the likes of myself a backing for a twenty-minute spot. In the year 1959, I opened The 59 Club in Hackney, East London, and some weeks later worked with Cliff at the official opening of the Club, with Princess Margaret in attendance, it was indeed a great night. I recall another memorable show we did with Cliff and The Shads; it was at The Edmonton Gaumont, North London. An afternoon show, with just Russ Sainty and The Nu-Notes performing the whole of the first half, and with Cliff and The Shadows doing the whole of the second half. It was one of those shows that went like a dream.

Over the years I've always kept in touch with members of The Shadows, and always tried to see their shows when on tour. We were all together of course recently in September 2006, when unveiling that historic plaque on the wall of the original 2 i's Coffee Bar in Soho London. Sadly, Tony Meehan, an early Shads drummer, was missing; he had passed away following an accident at home. Unfortunately, Hank Marvin couldn't make it from his home in Australia. However, as I've previously documented, Cliff gave a rousing speech, and a great day was had by all of us. I for one am always conscious of the fact that Cliff Richard and The Shadows led the way for many years in the pop group business; we all wanted to be like them. Cliff has been a great ambassador to the pop music world, and has stayed at the top for fifty years, a truly fantastic achievement. Sir Cliff Richard, a real star and real pop music phenomenon. I wonder why he never played at the 'Cali'?

CRAIG DOUGLAS

This gentleman is one of my closest friends in show business. We first met at the 'Cali' early in 1960 and again in the autumn of 1960, when Russ Sainty and The Nu-Notes were booked to do a three-week tour with Craig Douglas, Ricky Valance, The Mudlarks, Al Saxon, and one or two others. The Nu-Notes backed the whole show, which for them was a first and quite a big deal, but they did a great job and the tour was a big success. Craig, of course, had some big record successes, with numbers like "Only Sixteen", "Pretty Blue Eyes", "Hundred Pounds of Clay", "Lonesome Me", "When My Little Girl is Smiling" and quite a few more. Like Cliff Richard, Craig Douglas is a credit to our business, a real gentleman who is still performing and singing better than ever. Just before the cruise ship Canberra was de-commissioned, Craig, The Dallas Boys and I did a three-week booking on board, cruising around the Mediterranean, which was great fun.

I can also tell you that Craig Douglas is a great one for "popping in". Yes

Craig Douglas and myself get together at a recent show, Autumn 2007.

indeed whenever he's in the area, Craig will call in for a cuppa, and on a few occasions he has come back after his show and stayed the night, and we love to see him. So many people say they will call and see you, but never make it. Craig always finds the time and he knows that he is more than welcome in our house, at any time.

OLIVIA NEWTON JOHN

I had the great pleasure of meeting this lovely lady during the early 1970s. I had gone to see The Shadows performing at the Portsmouth Guildhall and, before the show started, I went back stage to see the Boys, and to my pleasant surprise, sitting with The Shads, was this very pretty young lady, Olivia Newton John. Bruce Welch introduced me to her saying, "Russ, keep her company whilst we do a sound check." I replied to Bruce, "Err, yeh, that won't be a problem, see you shortly." Of course, at that time Bruce was going steady with Olivia. She was charming to chat with, and I'm sure we covered both all her woes and mine. She told me how she was fed up and disillusioned with her show business career and talked about a return to Australia.

The Shads having finished their sound check, we all drifted into their dressing room, where I offered to pop out to a shop we then owned called "Ann's Bake 'n' Take" in Albert Road Portsmouth, to get them some chicken and chips, but after some "to-in and fro-in" they said ,"Russ, don't bother, but thanks anyway." I then said my goodbyes and went out front to watch the show. That was the first and last time I was to meet Olivia Newton John, but of course we all know what happened next. Yes, that's right, she had a hit record with a Bob Dylan song called "If Not for You" and her career took off; the rest is history, as the saying goes, from total disillusion to massive stardom, that's show business I guess!

Two shots of Ann's Bake 'n Take in Portsmouth, one of several take-away food outlets owned by Russ and Ann Sainty in the 1960s and '70s.

BERT WEEDON

Guitarist extraordinaire Bert, known as the man who taught the world to play guitar. His book, "Play in a Day", published in 1957, has sold well over two million copies all over the world, not forgetting his hit records, such as "Guitar Boogie Shuffle". I first met Bert Weedon when doing a BBC broadcast in 1960, but really got to know him during 1961, when I did many broadcasts without The Nu-Notes, and would use session musicians provided by the Beeb. Bert is a really lovely and charming man, and though in those early days I was completely lacking any experience of working with top musicians of the day, the likes of Kenny Clare (drums), Don Lusher (trombone), Rex Morris (tenor sax) and many more, Bert was always very patient and kind to me when rehearsing for the show. I continued to do dozens of BBC shows with Bert as band leader throughout the early sixties. It wasn't until 1983, when I was booked as Entertainments Manager for Warner Holidays, at their Sinah Warren Centre, that I once again met up with Bert, when he was booked for cabaret. I was then lucky enough to work with Bert Weedon for much of the 1980s at various venues around the country; however I have not seen him for many years now, though I know he is still out there, working and showing what a talented man he is, both as a guitarist and as an entertainer. Bert Weedon, another shining star!

KENNY BALL

Kenny with his Jazzmen were a great traditional band, believe me when you talk about a band "Swinging" these were the best! I worked alongside Kenny Ball and his band on the BBC Show, "Easy Beat", which was recorded on Wednesday evenings and broadcast on air, Sunday Mornings. Kenny Ball was resident on the show, so we would meet up at least once a month, since Russ Sainty and The Nu-Notes were regulars, but remember also that I would do shows without The Nu-Notes quite often. We got to know each other very well and would always have a drink in the pub just up the road from The Playhouse Theatre, where the show was recorded, not forgetting that Kenny was an Essex Boy, as indeed I am myself. During the early sixties, Kenny Ball and his Jazzmen made some great records like "Samantha" and "Midnight in Moscow", both big hits for the band.

I have not seen Kenny for many years, but I believe he is still working, giving his trumpet hell! Keep Swinging, Kenny!

LULU

I don't know her very well, but I did do a week's cabaret with her in the early 1970s, a big club in Rhyl, North Wales. We did get to chat on a few occasions, and I think it's fair to say, with Lulu, what you see is what you get; she was very nice to me, with a great bubbly personality, and she has been at the top since her first big hit record "Shout". Can't do much better than that!

BOBBY VEE

I had the pleasure of working with Bobby, when Russ Sainty and The Nu-Notes were booked to do a three-week tour with Bobby Vee, The Crickets, Ronnie Carroll and a few others in 1962. Once again, The Nu-Notes backed the whole show, but by now they were very experienced and made light work of what was quite a big job. Bobby was an extremely nice guy, and had enjoyed some big hit records at this time like, "Devil or Angel", "Rubber Ball", "Take Good Care Of My Baby" "More Than I Can Say" and "Run to Him". This was a most enjoyable tour, not only Bobby Vee, but The Crickets, who were our idols. We would all travel in a tour bus, so you can imagine the sort

of banter that went on amongst us all, with Ronnie Carroll always wanting to play cards, oh he did like a little flutter did Ronnie! During the 1990s I went to see Bobby Vee at The Portsmouth Guildhall. I was taken backstage, where we had a really happy meeting, talking about the tour we did in '62, and to my great surprise his son was playing drums in his backing group!

left Bobby Vee, a photo taken from Bobby 's programme when appearing at Portsmouth Guildhall in the 1980s. Note the advertisement of the first show Bobby did in England, 1962.

HELEN SHAPIRO

I first met Helen during a live BBC broadcast from The Royal Albert Hall in 1963. She was of course the youngest British female singer, at only 14 years old, to have two number one hits, in 1961, namely "Walkin' Back to Happiness" and "You Don't Know Me". We didn't meet up again until I was booked as her supporting act at Baileys Club, Stoke on Trent in the early 1970s; we were also booked into the same "pro digs", a place called The Flower Pot Hotel, which was not that special. We did get to chat a little, but in truth I always felt she was a little down in the dumps and didn't want to get into any real conversation. Following this period, she got into singing Jazz.

EDEN KANE

Had a couple of big hits in the year 1961, namely "Well I Ask You" and "Get Lost", followed in 1962 by the likes of "Forget Me Not" and "I Don't Know Why". Eden Kane, like Cliff Richard, was born in India, then came to England and found success as a Rock 'n' Roll singer. I met Eden whilst doing a TV Show in Cardiff in the year 1962; we were both plugging our new records, which in my case was "Send Me the Pillow". Strangely enough, neither of us had driven from London to Cardiff, we had both let the "train take the strain", as the saying goes. After the show, we had a meal together and got the sleeper train back to London; we chatted for a while, then both went our separate ways to find our beds. The next thing I remember was someone knocking on my carriage door telling me, I must now get off of the train. "Where are we?" I shouted to the guard. He replied "London, we have been in the station for an hour." Blimey, I've overslept, and in panic I quickly got myself dressed, grabbed my case and jumped off the train. The platform was empty, everyone had been long gone, including my girlfriend Ann, who was due to meet me on arrival but assumed I had missed the train and made her way to work in Bond Street. What a cock-up I've made, I was thinking, and made my way to get the tube train home to Leyton. I've never seen Eden Kane from that day to this. Though I guess it's never too late. I did, however, meet up again with Ann, my girlfriend. Then married her!

TOMMY STEELE

The first British Rock 'n' Roll Star, having hit the jack-pot with his 1956 hit recording of "Rock with the Caveman". Tommy, like myself, was born a "Cockney" south of the Thames, though I was born north of the Thames; we are also the same age, born in 1936, though I am a few months older than him, shame! My first encounter with Mr Steele was on a warm summer's evening, when myself and The Nu-Notes were waiting in Leicester Square for our pick up, taking us to an American Air base for a cabaret show. Tommy suddenly came flying along in a small sports car, which might have been an MG Midget, I'm not completely sure. Then, as he passed us, he drove straight at our band equipment, which was on the edge of the pavement, but as he swerved away shouted to us, "Have a great night fellows," and sped off, waving his arms frantically. My next encounter was early 1963; Tommy was preparing for the stage musical "Half a Sixpence". Myself and another young singer, called Barry Hopkins, were chosen to be Tommy Steele's understudies playing the part of Arthur Kipps. This was indeed a fabulous role to do and for me a big break. Now here, my dear reader, is a little teaser for you, and the clues are in the book! Was my part as understudy for Tommy, playing Arthur Kipps, fact or fiction? After all, I have been singing songs from the musical in my cabaret show, ever since the musical's opening in March 21st 1963, at The Cambridge Theatre, London.

Now, my thinking is that this would be the perfect time to call "Time" on this chapter. I have after all elsewhere in the book documented bits and bobs about many other stars and friends in the business. The likes of The Barron Knights, Brian Poole and The Tremeloes, Mike Berry, Shane Fenton (now Alvin Stardust) and so many more. However, let me close by answering a question that so many people have asked me over the years. "Russ, who have been your inspirations?" A good question and easily answered. With regard to my Rock 'n' Roll career, there are just two people, Elvis Presley and Ricky Nelson. With regard to inspiration in general – Freddy Laker, and just about anyone who makes GOOD, does GOOD and is GOOD!

THE CALI ALBUM
Life and Times at the California Ballroom, Dunstable

Diane Ilka

Hundreds of the now iconic pop stars of the sixties and seventies performed live at the unique California Ballroom in Dunstable. Thousands of their fans, local and nationwide, flocked to revel in the unforgettable atmosphere thus created.

Diane Ilka – granddaughter of the 'Cali's' founder – lived and worked
there. A generation on, she has compiled a tribute to this very special
phenomenon in pop music's history, including many pictures and contract details from her private collection of memorabilia. All those who
were part of the 'Cali' era can now reminisce over the stars and dates
that formed a highlight of their most impressionable years.

The 'Cali' lives on in the reunions and websites it still inspires. Now
it also has a fitting pictorial souvenir and record of those idols and
dreams of yesteryear.

A HATFUL OF MUSIC
The Dance Band Days in Luton, Dunstable & District

Stuart Goodyear

In 1939 Lutonian Stuart Goodyear was born into a musical household, whose father, also Stuart, encouraged him to embrace his love of music.

As a millennium project, Stuart was asked by the Luton Historical Society to write a page or two about the local "dance band days" of the last century, and drawing on his own involvement as novice pianist through to bandleader, was happy to undertake the challenge.

Starting in a modest way in the 1950s with fellow airport apprentices, his first band The Rainbow Melody Makers, rapidly became a larger and more polished dance band, and was subsequently renamed The Ray Miller Band. Remaining as leader of the band through to the 1980s, he became well connected with the local musical establishment, and has comprehensively collated his experiences during that time, although it soon became apparent that the finished article would be a book, rather than a dossier.

In a most fascinating personal and wider-ranging survey of musical days gone by in Luton, Dunstable and the surrounding area, Stuart has compiled a detailed impression of how he remembered the busy dance scene, and the many brilliant musicians who contributed to a period of live musical entertainment that will never return.

Deliberating over a title, he shortlisted "Batons and Bows" and "You've Gotta Lot to Learn My Boy", but thinks that "A Hatful of Music" just about strikes the right chord. The book contains over 300 photos of events covered over the years. People born and bred in Luton will be pouring over the nostalgia for weeks to come.

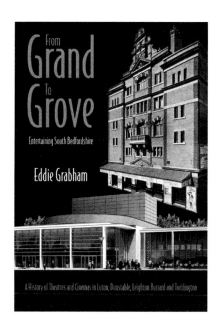

FROM GRAND TO GROVE
A History of Theatres and Cinemas in Luton, Dunstable, Leighton Buzzard and Toddington

Eddie Grabham

The people of Dunstable, Leighton Buzzard and Luton have been entertained for centuries. The first purpose-built theatre opened in 1898, but the first dramatic performance can be traced back to the twelfth century.

This book explores the travelling players, the fit-ups, weekly rep, variety, one-night stands, pop concerts, and the buildings they occupied. It tells the story of early film shows, small cinemas before the movies could talk, the cine-variety theatres, the super cinemas and the multiplexes.

The area covered is a diverse one, ranging from the urbanised bustle of Luton to the rural calm of Toddington. It is interesting to note how such diversity has caused South Bedfordshire to be typical of provincial areas outside the major cities and metropolitan centres for artistic endeavour as well as stage and screen entertainment.

It all adds up to a fascinating history of early enterprise, dramatic fires, bitter competition and a host of famous stars of stage and screen whose one mission was to entertain South Bedfordshire. There were times when the development of the theatres and cinemas provided drama every bit as exciting as that seen on stage or screen.

Book Castle PUBLISHING

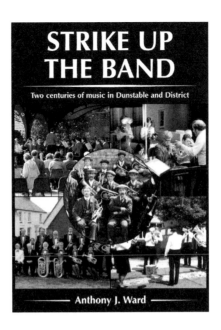

STRIKE UP THE BAND
Two centuries of music in Dunstable and District

Anthony J. Ward

In 'Strike Up The Band', the author traces the history of music-making in Dunstable and District from the earliest times where information is available, up to the present day. It is derived from a wider ongoing project by the author.

The book particularly emphasises the history and development of Brass Bands, Orchestras and other groups, recording their contributions to the changing life of the Town and District, and highlighting the various celebrations that have taken place over so many years. The book closes with a series of chapters on the three local Senior Schools in Dunstable with their bands, orchestras and music.

The design of the book is largely based on a collection of photographs and memorabilia, derived from the wide number of contributors having connections with the organisations featured in the book, featuring their recollections of events and personalities. The story of music-making in Dunstable and its surrounding villages is shown in the context of the history of the area and its citizens.

Book Castle
PUBLISHING

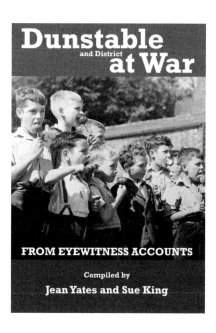

DUNSTABLE AND DISTRICT AT WAR
From Eyewitness Accounts

Compiled by Jean Yates and Sue King

Dunstable and District at War is mainly a collection of personal reminiscences, by people who lived here or who called Dunstable home during the Second World War. Hundreds of recent interviews have recaptured these unique memories that evoke the disrupted, day-to-day life of an archetypal rural town in that unique period of British history. Bedfordshire was at the heart of the Secret War and Dunstable was very much a part of it. The Meteorological Office was based at the bottom of the Downs, and forecasters worked closely with Bomber Command to decide the date for D-Day.

This book tries to give a feel for where Dunstable sat in the wider picture; the relationships it had and the part it played in conjunction with Bletchley Park, Black Propaganda, SOE and our Allies. There is also a section about those of our Allies who sought refuge in Dunstable after the war. And a final chapter recounts a few of the remarkable contributions Dunstablians made to the various battlefronts overseas, including D-Day and the Far East.

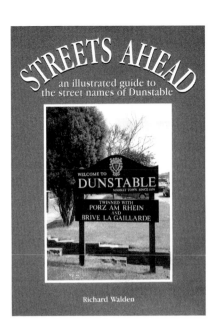

STREETS AHEAD
An illustrated guide to the street names of Dunstable

Richard Walden

Over the past 150 years Dunstable has expanded from a small rural market town with limited development beyond the four main streets, to a modern urban town of 35,000 inhabitants and over 400 individual streets. The names of many of these streets have been carefully chosen for some specific reason. Dunstable's modern housing estates in particular have been spared the all too common anonymity of poets, painters, authors and birds found in most other towns. In Dunstable, developers and the local Council have taken great care to select names which record elements of the town's unique historical past and some of the characters and events which helped shape the local community.

Based upon a series of articles written for the Dunstable Gazette in 1992/94, Richard Walden has considerably expanded his text to include details, where known, of every street in the town to date of publication. As much of Dunstable has been developed only in this century, *Streets Ahead* with its numerous illustrations is also a fascinating record of the town's recent history.